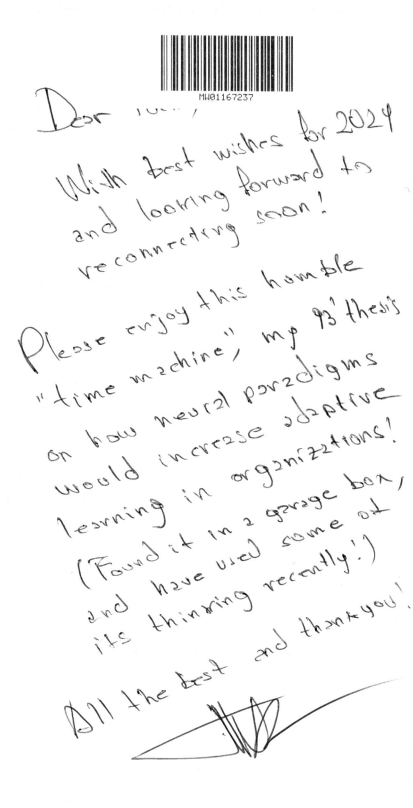

Dear ...

With best wishes for 2024 and looking forward to reconnecting soon!

Please enjoy this humble "time machine", my B' thesis on how neural paradigms would increase adaptive learning in organizations! (Found it in a garage box, and have used some of its thinking recently!)

All the best and thank you!

THE DESIGN OF LEARNING ORGANIZATIONS

THE DESIGN OF LEARNING ORGANIZATIONS

EMBRACING THE NEURAL NETWORK PARADIGM OF

COLLECTIVE LEARNING ACROSS THE ORGANIZATION

Picos, Alex (Alejandro)
The Design of Learning Organizations: Embracing the Neural Network Paradigm of Collective Learning across the Organization / Alex Picos

ISBN: 9798872298120
271 Pages
1. New Business Designs. 2. Artificial Intelligence. 3. Collaborative Human-Machine Learning. 4. Organization. 5. Diffusion of Innovation

Printed and bound in the USA by Intellixens LLC

Graphics by Alexander Gaspar Picos and Vanina Bruno
Illustrations by Alexander Gaspar Picos and Vanina Bruno
Jacket Design by Alex Picos and Vanina Bruno

1st printing

Second Edition

To the loving memory of my parents,
Maria Luisa Losada de Picos and Gaspar Picos Calvo

And to my beloved wife and son,
Brigida Picos and Alexander Gaspar Picos

Content

THE DESIGN OF
LEARNING
ORGANIZATIONS

Preface

1993 AI-DRIVEN THOUGHTS

Why does a 30-year time capsule matter?

J UNE 27ᵀᴴ, 1993. That day, I printed out the final page of my MBA thesis, which is in your hands thirty years later. The world stood then on the brink of IT wonders, though few truly understood the sheer magnitude of the revolution laying ahead of us. I was but a young Electronics Engineer, fresh off the tidal wave of the personal computer's inception. Amidst the era's mainstream novelties, I was captivated by something way more intriguing: *neural networks*. Experimental and esoteric, I persuaded my manager at IBM to send me to the 2ⁿᵈ Neural Network Congress in Paris in 1990, *returning convinced that this was the future.*

A world where systems would evolve in symbiosis with human cognition. Businesses would have to reshape their very fabric to align with AI's pulsating heartbeat.

The *Design of Learning Organizations* is about that brave future, envisioned back then: *Humans leveraging AI models, self-organizing in novel ways to mimic a collective brain, its main goal being becoming smarter, faster, and better.*

My early working days were filled with advanced mainframes and complex oil and gas reservoir simulations. *It became clear to me then the great potential computing technology had, beyond mere ledger-processing.* That perception was reinforced by my later MBA journey at IESA and Cornell, where I was drawn into the realms of Strategy, Economics, and Organizational Design.

I saw a gap back then, where technology was seen just as a tool but not as a major driver of an entirely new paradigm. Those days, *I somehow daydreamt of organizations that mirrored the human brain, possessing sensory, motor, and control capabilities, constantly learning and adapting at a speed we had never imagined.*

Yet, the stark reality was that most companies back then, as many still do now, stifled innovation. The data-rich insights that could propel them were ignored; only accounting records seemed to matter. After my MBA, I joined McKinsey & Co., a Firm thriving on learning and collaboration. I was gifted an ideal canvas to experiment in strategic IT, culminating in co-leading the launch of what today became McKinsey Digital.

Fast forward to my Fintech career and global endeavors with PayPal, and I found myself at the helm of a realization. The neural models and generative technologies that were once figments of imagination, had matured. It is not just about enabling efficiency goals anymore, but unleashing the reshaping of businesses, processes, and human interaction, benefiting anyone embracing collective learning paradigms.

This book encapsulates the musings and dreams of a young MBA student, *with a deep technical background and just a few years of experiences under his belt,* living in a distant land back then, facing challenges like a heart-breaking unfulfilled Stanford graduate admission due to a direct familial loss. *My hope is that it will mirror the aspirations of countless 'smart creatives', who at any level or anywhere, see every day a brave and boundless digital future.*

If my humble vision then, is fueling a great journey, I cannot but imagine the possibilities ahead of all of us. We are scratching the surface of an effort reshaping humanity at all levels: individual, societal, generational.

While you embark on this reading, I encourage you to embrace the untouched, 30-year-old references and academic jargon, as charming anchors to a bygone era. Please immerse in *what turned out to be enduring principles,* which to my own surprise may be more relevant today than back then.

Also, as you sift through this thesis, accidentally found in storage after all this years, *please look forward to a sequel that will build on the principles exposed, updating them to our present experience, to ponder the Generative AI prospects ahead of us.* Leaders of all types can harness the renewed promise of AI and uplift collective learning. *We are still in the infancy of the symbiosis between AI and human era — it is just 2023!*

Thank you for embarking on this journey. Please share your insights, which are invaluable as we face unprecedented change. *A world of enlightenment, beckoning us to shape the future.*

Warmly,

Alex Picos

Boca Raton, FL
& Palo Alto, CA
2023

Introduction

THE DESIGN OF LEARNING ORGANIZATIONS
The Neural Paradigm of Collective Learning

T HE LANDSCAPE OF ORGANIZATIONAL STUDIES is increasingly populated with terms that were once infrequently employed, such as *organizational learning, intelligent companies, and institutional memory.*

References to learning processes within organizations are beginning to appear more frequently in both the managerial and academic worlds.

This trend meets an increasing demand, as evidenced by the popularity of works from pioneers like Chris Argyris[1], through to today's bestsellers such as Senge's *The Fifth Discipline*[2], prominently displayed alongside cash registers in leading bookstores everywhere.

What drives this shared interest among researchers and managers? Is it merely a passing trend or a new paradigm poised to revolutionize our current understanding of organizations?

4

ORGANIZATIONAL LEARNING:
THE ULTIMATE COMPETITIVE ADVANTAGE

A central premise of this work is that the ability to learn and adapt is the ultimate critical competitive asset for most companies. *This trend is not a fad; it's here to stay.*

Consequently, several critical questions arise for executives, consultants and academics:

1) The Intent Question:
   Is enhancing collective learning really that important?
2) The Feasibility Question:
   Is it possible to enhance an organization's learning abilities? Can we accelerate collective learning 'by design'?
3) The Design Question:
   If so, how can this be done? Can organizational structures be rearranged to maximize learning, compared with others? How would this approach differ from traditional practices?
4) The People Question:
   Can staff be retrained? If so, how, and what training programs would be most effective? What traits matter the most?
5) The Technology Question:
   How to best organize technology and applications to support collective organizational learning?

In response to these pressing questions, *the objective of this work is to make the case for a new collective learning paradigm, proposing an organizational design methodology to address this need.*

This work is conceived to assist empowered agents, *(executives, managers, consultants, or academics)* seeking to improve collective learning capabilities.

Our motivation is derived from a noticeable gap in the study of learning structures within organizations. *This field has yet to incorporate the latest advances in information processing,* offering the possibility of structuring collective learning, paired with supportive structural designs and feedback systems.

To begin with, we will propose *an operationalizable definition of organizational learning,* which will draw on the latest developments in brain science.

Subsequently, we will explore *collective learning diagnostic tools* for practitioners, to anchor the desired objectives.

Following this stage, the foundations of collective learning will be analyzed, drawing inspiration from breakthroughs in the computational field of Artificial Neural Networks.

Finally, implementation recommendations will be provided to address the enhancement of collective learning by designing better structures and adaptive supporting systems.

***

There is no valid reason to stick to XIX century 'Industrial Revolution' functional designs. The IT revolution is here to stay, and companies must embrace novel ways to structure themselves, train their staff and strategize around learning.

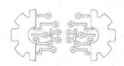

1

ORGANIZATIONAL LEARNING

Is it just an intangible factor?

T HE FIRST OBSTACLE SCHOLARS FACE when researching organizational learning is the lack of a concrete, actionable definition for the term. Though one might assume that the meaning of 'learning' is self-evident, its implications differ depending on context and often lean toward individual rather than collective learning. Even authoritative dictionaries fall short in capturing its nuance and offer definitions riddled with contradictions:

To learn *(from Lat. apprehendere):* tr. To acquire knowledge of something through study or experience. | | To conceive something based on mere appearances or with little foundation. | | To store something in memory. | | To apprehend. | | To teach, transmit knowledge[1]

To complicate matters, over time, leading academics have viewed organizational learning predominantly as an individual-centric process: Pivotal jobholders take on learning initiatives, challenge existing paradigms in search of better solutions, and rally their colleagues around a vision for transformation.

TIMELINE:
ORGANIZATIONAL LEARNING RESEARCH

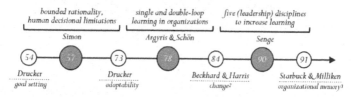

While these frameworks had immense value, *they somehow fall short of providing definitions for collective, organizational learning.* The underlying assumption was that a critical mass of skilled individuals, homegrown or brought in, is essential for driving superior organizational learning.

This idea may be valid in old-fashioned military-style organizations, where carefully organized 'chains of command' rely on highly centralized headquarters. In doing so, research may be perpetuating a potential, unintended, fallacy:

PERCEPTION:
SMART PEOPLE PROPEL TEAM LEARNING

One common misperception about organizational learning is that it is simply an extension of individual learning. While it's true that individual learning is a necessary component, organizational learning is more complex, involving a structural approach to collectively create and improve organizational knowledge.

REALITY:
GROUPTHINK STIFFLES LEARNING

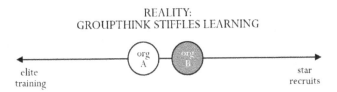

Indeed, *one of the most insidious barriers to approach collective learning seems to lie in organizational dynamics and structures.* As we deep-dive into corporate interactions, the reality is that *groupthink[4],* short-term results, and political maneuvers often paralyze its potential. These factors not only suppress facts and dissenting viewpoints but also muffle innovative ideas.

The irony here is that organizations, originally designed to seek competitive results, become learning mazes that trap innovation. This compromises the quality of collective decision-making, often suboptimal compared to the capabilities of its members.

Now, as we navigate this complex landscape, we find invaluable scholarly insights into how individuals and their support systems are challenged to learn within an organization.

The next section will peruse through some of these works, verify their focus on individual learning, *and propose a paradigm-shift, centered on a revised definition of collective learning.*

DECODING THE LEARNING MAZE

Nobel laureate and Carnegie-Mellon Professor Herbert Simon[5] was among the early contributors to this topic. His concept of *bounded rationality* is paramount: In decision-making, humans face limits in terms of information, cognitive limitations, and time.

As a result, *we cannot optimize but rather satisfice, that is, humans just seek a good-enough solution given the circumstances, rather than an optimal one.*

HUMAN DECISION PROCESS (OFTEN SUBOPTIMAL)

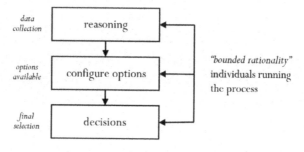

This view posits that organizational learning stems from individual experiences, amalgamated via the organization's communication system, with memories stored in human minds or archives.

This thesis called for further exploration of the way in which individual learning persists within an organization, somehow placing the emphasis on individuals as the key learning entities driving the learning process, despite their limitations.

Conversely, Harvard scholar Chris Argyris and MIT's Donald Schön[6] depict organizational learning as a process that navigates barriers at both the individual and collective levels.

Humans appear to generate organizational lessons, by making decisions, either within competitive or collaborative environments:

DOUBLE LOOP LEARNING (CODIFIED IN VALUES)

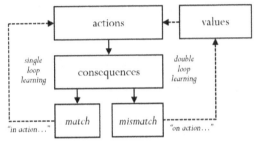

Their proposed learning process has two modalities:

- *simple loop, adapting behaviors to achieve desired results,* and
- *double loop, probing deeper into improvement opportunities.*

Schön's concepts of live *'reflection-in-action'* and evaluative *'reflection-on-action'* integrate well into this framework.

However these still reaffirm that organizational learning stems from individual experiences and does not address how these reflections get documented.

Do these insights become part of the organizational culture? Are they codified in procedural manuals? Or, will they reside solely in the minds of the employees involved in the reflective processes?

Regardless of the modality, *individuals continue to learn independently and occasionally share their findings.* Unfortunately, it is often the results, rather than the learning process, that determine rewards, *irrespective of the quality of these exchanges.*

Lastly, Peter Senge, also from MIT, offers another perspective. His bestselling work, *The Fifth Discipline*[7], proposes a way to boost organizational learning, advocating for *a shared systemic vision, team values, and individual learning.*

He argues that the ability to create *mental models* to engage in *systems thinking,* is the way to perfect the organization's system, evading negative dynamics that get in the way of improvement.

ADDRESSING ROOT CAUSES, NOT SYMPTOMS

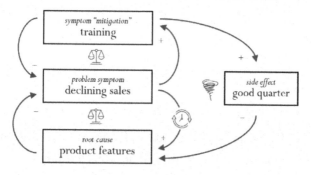

In this view, a physical model, depicting all the variables at play and relations between them, is crucial for gaining collective insights and drive adaptation. However, the question of who set up such models, evaluate their performance and organize the execution remains open. Sometimes this capability may be externalized to consultants.

A CROSS-DISCIPLINARY DEFINITION

Nearly all definitions of collective learning we could source to date, in organizational theory, consist of descriptions of the results obtained by individual learning, shared through pre-set channels *(subjectively depicted conforming upon each author's perspective).*

An alternative would be to reflect on the way stimuli collection, input processing and corresponding new insights and actions occur at the collective level.

Institutional learning so defined, would not be dependent on any entity to keep configuring a highly adaptive network.

The novelty of this topic in organizational studies indicates a need for input, ideas, and frameworks from other domains to define collective learning effectively

Are there other scientific disciplines that have formally studied learning and decomposed it as a process?

Learning has been intensely studied within psychology, biological, and computational sciences. When it comes to its inner works, most research focuses on how simple neurons within the brain interact in a networked way and drive collective learning.

Insights from these diverse fields can be applied to the organizational context where, at its core, the organization as an entity reflects characteristics derived from the behavior of its members.

MULTIPLE SCIENTIFIC DISCIPLINES INTERACTING

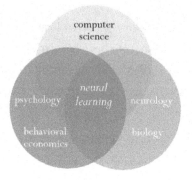

Organizations are often described with human-like qualities: capricious, perverse, formal, careless, creative, or excellent – just as one would refer to a close friend's personality.

What if a collective brain of sorts is formed somewhat independently of the individual learning experiences of the organization members, by connecting their outputs *(thoughts, decisions, actions)* in a way that yields unique, collective insights, knowledge, and approaches to situations?

This perspective also allows us to consider characterizing organizations as 'brilliant' when they adapt rapidly and 'dull' when they do not. While all entities surely rely on the learning characteristic of their individual members, it is their structural connectivity and arrangement that most significantly drive varying organizational learning profiles.

The following definition is proposed:

> **Organizational learning:** Process through which an organization acquires the ability to respond appropriately to situations it may or may not have previously encountered. || Favorable modification of the organization's reaction tendencies, thanks to the processing of prior experiences, particularly the construction of new formalized organizational routines. || Storage of events in organizational memory, so they can be retrieved in a format that allows situational processing.

NOT 'YET ANOTHER DEFINITION'

Under this paradigm, organizational learning is not merely a buzzword; it is a critical enterprise function that enables better adaptation to ever-changing environmental conditions.

The key to this approach is to look beyond individual human learning and focus on the network effects of information exchanges across the structure. *Specifically, we should examine:*

a) How *situations, old and new, are collectively processed,* adapting operational responses based on experience,

b) Whether *these adaptation routines are continually assessed* and formalized according to their level of success,

c) What *kind of storage structures and systems are available* to support some form of shared memory

At its primary level, organizational learning manifests itself as a *gestalt,* enabling individuals to formulate and jointly assess various scenarios. This approach facilitates shared solutions to efficiently address new, complex situations.

At a more advanced level, it includes continuously assessing the performance of these primary adaptation procedures. This process includes reinforcing successful primary learning mechanisms and phasing out less effective ones.

Finally, a clearly defined construct, featuring appropriate systems, should be capable of storing events and outcomes. *Reliable memories are essential for the evolving learning process.*

This brings us to a central proposition: *the existence of an Organizational Learning System,* beyond individual learning, in all entities. Informal or formal, highly functioning, or not, any group of individuals interacting in an organization establish collective knowledge separate from their own experience.

ORGANIZATIONAL LEARNING SYSTEM

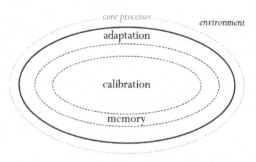

16

Under this view, organizational learning encompasses a process far broader than mere individual habit formation and sharing.

It can be structured as a vital function, and its processes and systems be designed, documented, and measured in terms of efficiency, with metrics such as adaptation speed, error reduction, efficiency in resource utilization, and improved outcomes.

The potential to propel break-through results, elevates this asset, from a 'soft', intangible factor to a powerful force, able to shape the enterprise competitiveness, particularly in times of turmoil. When properly understood, designed, and implemented, it becomes a game-changer, differentiating successful, adaptive companies from those destined for obsolescence.

***

In a world evolving faster than ever, can any leader afford to ignore the tangible value of increasing their organization's learning rate? Let's explore that issue next.

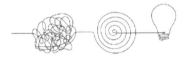

2

COMPETITIVENESS AND LEARNING

Are they strongly correlated?

B EFORE WE ADDRESS THE DESIGN PROCESS of organizational learning, it's essential to reflect on the significance of this capability. *Is pursuing this concept relevant at all? Why could fostering collective learning be so important? Does it correlate with company performance?* Let's examine some evidence to assess the potential benefits and value of this process.

To assess the relationship between learning and strategic competitiveness, we conducted an analysis of the most impactful articles published in *Harvard Business Review (HBR)*, a journal that has set the gold standard for thought leadership in corporate strategy. Utilizing LexisNexis view statistics, sourced from Cornell University's Johnson School Library, we chose the top 10 most-searched articles over the past 15 years.

We reviewed each work to determine whether it addressed organizational or individual dynamics, and reviewed its content for mentions of learning as a key attribute.

HBR MOST INFLUENTIAL ARTICLES (1978-1993)

rank	title	author	yr	focus	mentions learning
1	The Five Competitive Forces That Shape Strategy[1]	Porter	79	organizational	no
2	Strategic Intent[2]	Hamel & Prahalad	89	organizational	yes
3	The Balanced Scorecard, Measures That Drive Performance[3]	Kaplan & Norton	92	organizational	no
4	Kaizen: The Key To Japan's Competitive Success	Imai	86	organizational	yes
7	The New New Product Development Game[7]	Takeuchi & Nonaka	86	organizational	yes
5	The Discipline of Teams[5]	Katzenbach & Smith	93	organizational	no
9	Managing Brand Equity[9]	Aaker	91	organizational	no
8	Competing on Capabilities: The New Rules of Corporate Strategy[8]	Stalk, Evans & Shulman	92	organizational	no
4	Teaching Smart People How to Learn[4]	Argyris	91	individual	yes
10	The Globalization of Markets[10]	Levitt	83	organizational	no

The results are revealing: three of the top ten HBR blockbuster articles, commonly used in MBA *curricula* around the world, explicitly emphasize how key team learning is.

Moreover, those three articles had something else in common: They focused on competitiveness. Specifically, they addressed *why American corporations seem to be losing their edge to*

Japanese firms, due to better products and strategies, all stemming from accelerated learning practices.

COMPANY LEARNING APPROACHES: US VS JAPAN

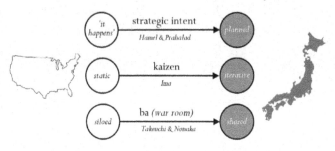

A new strategic competitiveness paradigm is emerging. Nowadays, companies like Sony, Canon, Fujitsu, Toyota, and Komatsu *(among many others)* are under the world's microscope, eager to dissect their seemingly unstoppable success formula.

TO LEARN OR NOT TO LEARN?
THAT IS THE QUESTION...

Hamel and Prahalad's work is emerging as one of the most influential, rivalling Porter's approach to developing competitive advantage, offering a more 'adaptive' perspective.

Their work proposes a new competitive asset, displayed by novel Japanese global leaders: *A strategic intent vision, resulting in accelerated learning journeys to master new core competencies.*

In their article, *Strategic Intent* [2], they detail how successful companies break down ambitious visions into a series of short and medium-term challenges to acquire key core competencies that will make a difference in terms of driving global competitiveness.

Their case studies on Honda, Komatsu, and Canon, *once humble, aspiring players in Japan*, document the mobilization of these players to master skills required to lead in their markets.

Other scholars focused on additional blockbuster Japanese cases, while many other examples flourished under the radar:

- Additional well-known global consumer cases include:
  - Sony's prowess in world-class innovation at affordable prices *(Walkman, Trinitron TVs, Laser Mini Discs)*
  - Most Japanese automakers *(Toyota, Nissan, Mitsubishi)*, featuring novel production and R&D practices
- Less documented examples, but equally disruptive, feature:
  - Fujitsu's startling development of IBM Mainframe clones *(FACOM series, powerful and lower costs)*
  - Panasonic's HDS7700 high-end computing storage, more advanced and resilient than other offerings
  - Fanuc's robotics *(along with Mazak, Okuma, and Mori)* fueled a revolution in Japan's manufacturing across sectors. *Yonex, ASICS, Uniqlo, Fuji, NEC* jumped at the opportunity *(sports apparel, chemicals, telecoms...)*

Entire industries are being disrupted by these companies, the reasons behind their success are a subject of ongoing debate. Hamel and Prahalad attribute it mainly to a clear top-down corporate vision, while Imai's work aligns their success with bottom-up improvements, achieved by *kaizen* circles on the shop floor.

Digging deeper, more perspectives emerge. Deming's[11] '14 Points' framework nurtured a seemingly indelible emphasis on quality improvement. Takeuchi and Nonaka[5] theorized about a potential direct consequence of that legacy: the emergence of robust knowledge management systems across these practices.

In our view, all these case studies reflect one thing in common: *accelerated organizational learning, as we defined it:*

- Capital-intensive players learned manufacturing technologies faster, to build better products, more efficiently (e.g. automakers, robot manufacturers, high-end computing)

- High-tech consumer providers leveraged shared consumer knowledge across units to create new 'use cases' for killer products (e.g. media & entertainment, office equipment)

- Other manufacturing industries perfected self-improvement, enabling 'fast retailing', catering to segments starving for the ultimate edge (e.g., sporting *goods, clothing retail)*

The similarities in their superior outcomes are remarkable when comparing each company to its global incumbents:

	Global 'incumbents' 'Big 3' High-Tech … Manufacturing		Japanese 'attackers' 'Big 3' High-Tech … Manufacturing	
cost to operate	*higher*		lower	
reliability	*lower*	*high / variable*	higher	raising
price	*higher*		lower	
dominant technology	*legacy*		VHC	*precision hydraulics*	*digital*

Upon reviewing the cases in literature *and those assessed through direct exposure, we postulate their common attribute is a structural, high organizational learning rate.*

All of these players have documented strategies and crafted specific charters *to invest and increase their learning rate on critical core skills, while summoning all the organization to leverage these efforts in a collaborative manner.*

In every case, we can trace to a higher learning rate *(materials, design, manufacturing process, customer insights)* with outstanding strategic outcomes.

'I See Only One Thing: The Enemy's Main Strength…'
— BRIGADIER GENERAL BONAPARTE, MILAN, 1797 [12]

The results of that accelerated, targeted learning, ultimately tipped the scales in favor of the winning companies. We call that a *catalyzed learning cycle,* in which shared strategic intent, short-circuits organizational boundaries, and accelerates resource allocation to increase

THE DESIGN OF LEARNING ORGANIZATIONS

experimentation in a way that is entirely aligned with the key market drivers. In Senge's modelling terms:

COMPANY LEARNING APPROACHES: US VS JAPAN

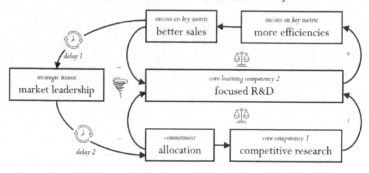

Specifically, in our view, the higher intrinsic learning rate in these organizations is achieved by:

1) Learning *'what to learn about'*: competitive research
    -   Markets rule, it is indeed critical to cater to their needs. *'What to learn,'* the competencies that produce products that will tilt the market away from competitors

    -   With record gas prices, do drivers care about engine power or mileage? *Cost of Ownership...*

    -   With all these PCs in the office, do we need high-maintenance copiers or more printers? *Reliability...*

    -   With high interest rates, will capital-intensive sectors like construction favor lower prices vs quality? *Price...*

2) Improving *'how to learn'*: excelling at critical R&D

- Highly coveted *know-how:* processes, formulas, systems. *'How to learn,' empowering all teams to innovate and improve constantly the chosen core competencies, at world class level*

- Can we produce a 40-mpg car, when the US standard is 25-30mpg? *Create a self-tuning engine: VTEC*

- Can our camera optoelectronics skills help scan the documents, and print them out? *Develop digital copiers...*

- Can smaller hydraulics help reduce equipment costs, be a better deal? *New load-sensing hydraulics: CLSS*

These features align quite well with our definition of Organizational Learning: a) *Jointly assessing situations across functions, and b) engaging in ongoing learning improvements.*

'From the Sublime to the Ridiculous is but a Step'
– NAPOLEON, EXILED EMPEROR OF ELBA, 1814 12

Let's look at the other side of the coin. Former market leaders, the incumbents, experienced an inverse process, sort of a 'learning death spiral'.

Threatened organizations tried to ignore the crisis, generating only partial and delayed responses that often only exacerbated the root-cause of the problems they were facing.

Soon, the entire corporation faces a degenerative process, typically driven by the need to cut R&D costs to 'improve' competitiveness, causing underinvestment in the organization's capacity and speed to generate or improve core competencies.

THE 'LEARNING DEATH' SPIRAL

Further cuts in sales incentives may drive salesforce attrition, delaying further needed market information to improve the product in meaningful ways. This may result in further workforce cuts, accelerating the erosion of core competencies, and foregoing the drive to innovate altogether.

This higher attrition fuels collective memory loss. Worker's tenure at US companies is declining: 4.3 years, compared to 8.6 years in Japan, according to the 1992 AMA survey.[13]

This leads us to a third feature, *the ability to retain and apply past knowledge,* also fueling the higher learning rate in these cases:

3) Leveraging 'prior knowledge': tapping on past learnings Lessons and skills gained through experience appear to be never taken for granted in great companies. *Au contraire,* they are at the center of all learning tables.

- Once a small motorcycle shop, *Honda drew learnings on bike motor design* to create more efficient car engines

- Canon not *only* leveraged camera optics, but deep consumer roots to grasp the personal copier market.

- Komatsu's military logistics heritage, enabled custom shops around the world

This last feature underscores our third Organizational Learning definition pillar: Memory. *Balancing existing memories and new adaptive options is crucial for learning.*

Consequently, incumbents plagued with low learning rates, poor functional connectivity, and the absence of mechanisms to counteract organizational amnesia have marked the decline of industrial giants like General Motors, resulting in temporary chaos and inordinate losses.

Which takes us to this section's impending question: *Is there a tangible economic value of learning?*

TRANSLATING LEARNING INTO EARNINGS

In all the cases portrayed in the article, there is a common thread: a great difference in value creation by companies with heightened learning rates and their competitive peer group.

Take Canon's example: While doing well in a very competed camera market, when combining world-class opto-electronics learning skills, with their strength capturing consumer's desires, resulted in amazing value creation, overtaking mighty incumbents like Xerox, in their own turfs.

THE VALUE OF COLLECTIVE LEARNING AT CANON

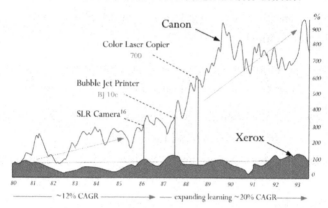

While obviously there are several other factors at play, *Canon's collective intelligence augmentation during this period is remarkable:* Enhanced situational perception, extraction of key features to compete on, using past learnings, and adapting distribution to operate across brand-new sectors.

Similar valuation stories underpin all these case studies, marked by inflection points when their learning systems were operating at peak. For example, Honda taking the lead in fuel efficiency triggered unforeseen US market gains:

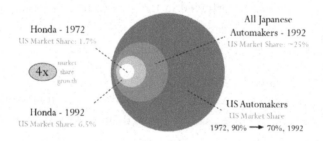

The global scene is not different. There are enormous share gains being captured by high-learning automakers, which adapted their product lines to the 1973's gas price hikes, depriving former leaders, slower to adapt, of their global dominance.

Finally, one last example of *'learning into earnings'*: Komatsu[20] has doubled its global share, largely at the expense of Caterpillar's. As we mentioned before, they did so by researching advanced hydraulics, in particular a variable flow system that would allow them to produce smaller formats and address new market niches.

By exploiting every advantage of their nimble technology, they went on customizing the equipment, manufacturing it right next to their customers.

The results of this learnings? 'Unbeatable' products in very attractive niche markets, such as mining and agriculture in Brazil, leveraging their core new technology, while enabling custom features.

Enabling their lighter equipment to handle precision jobs in small mining shafts or the muddiest farmlands from Mato Grosso to Parana, this input from the local communities was critical to best adapt their products.

Replicating this formula across markets, they achieved outstanding growth results, in very profitable, underserved segments that their competitors could not address.

KOMATSU'S 20 YEARS JOURNEY 'FROM 1 TO 20'

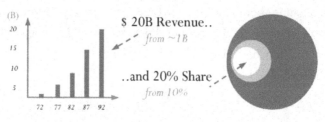

Therefore, the economic impact of organizational learning is well established. Companies that understand their markets more deeply, innovate faster, manufacture better and refine their 'go to market strategies' in a connected way, leveraging their past learnings, simply do better. *Way better.*

But does this hold true for companies of all sizes? Most of these cases involve players with significant critical mass, often tens of thousands of employees. Can these lessons be applied to smaller entities?

DAVIDS LEARN FASTER THAN GOLIATHS

The examples we find in literature are often those of large multinational companies competing for supremacy in global markets. However, this does not mean that small and medium businesses (SMBs) cannot benefit from organizational learning in a similar manner.

On the contrary, the structural mechanisms that promote learning are often easier and less expensive to implement in the context of a smaller organization, as most of these giants were at a point in their past.

Since their inception, the companies mentioned have cultivated procedures that favor the development of organizational heuristics and sharing data across all levels, thereby fostering a multitude of analytical processes that shorten product launches that markets love, while yielding defect-free, more efficient outcomes.

In the 1960s, most of these players were small, local manufacturers, striving to serve a depleted market. Consumers sought small, affordable goods to satisfy their needs, and larger infrastructure projects were scarce, as post-war Japan was being rebuilt on a budget. These companies faced struggles, maneuvering within an initially depleted ecosystem.

Perhaps their *high capacity for learning was developed when struggling as small players in their respective local ecosystems.* This attribute, in turn, transformed them into global leaders.

SURVIVAL OF THE SMARTEST

There seems to be a new competitive order that defies the locality of Porter's framework. In that view of competitiveness, highly successful organizations brew in places where there is a confluence of five forces *(buyer and supplier power, new entrants, substitute threats and competitive rivalry)*, typically in close geographical proximity to each other.

A brilliant work, resulting in some of the most influential managerial thinking of our time, shaping our views around the drivers of strategy. Environmental factors appear to create a brewing lab where core processes and supporting functions are shaped accordingly to the availability of talent to resource them in that ecosystem.

As a result of those catalysts, global leaders emerge, be it in the luxury handbag industry in Milan, or the high-tech industry in Silicon Valley. World-class leaders appear to be shaped by the strength of their environment.

However, what caused the downfall of Detroit? A world-class hub of automotive innovation that should be firing in all cylinders...

Every case study depicting organizations that are learning faster now, seems to be replacing in the competitive ecosystem a former 'fast learner', often hatched in these closely knitted innovation hubs.

Is learning a key competitive feature, derived from the environment, yet one that is hard to sustain?

Or, alternatively, is it a mere temporary conduct of aligned executives, supporting a rallied 'intent cry' emanating from the top?

We believe that companies which are able to lock in learning systems and structures succeed in creating sustainable organizational learning rates during longer periods of time.

We also think that a high concentration of learning entities in one physical place or market creates competition for talent, and these cross-pollination of practices results in the *(sometimes accidental)* acceleration of collective learning.

As more competing organizations enhance their learning capabilities, these internal changes will manifest in the environment: An increasing number of intelligent participants will soon change market competitive learning thresholds.

More competitive products and services, better aligned with consumer needs, will make survival harder for poorly adapted participants. Consequently, over time, the decision whether or not to improve an organization's learning capacity could trigger 'Darwinian' consequences: *Either learn or face extinction, potentially becoming a case study in a future 'organizational paleontology' article.*

> The capacity to learn effectively becomes a vital survival skill for companies, underscoring our axiom:
>
> *Learn how to collectively learn faster and better and thrive, or face decline and fade away.*

The question we now face is whether organizational learning can be intentionally designed, improved through sustainable structures, mechanisms, and systems, and nurtured as an enduring, core competency in its own right.

***

Exploring that possibility, *evolving learning by design,* will be the focus of the subsequent section.

3

LEARNING 'BY DESIGN'
Can we improve organizational learning?

A CKNOWLEDGING THE SIGNIFICANCE of learning for organizational success, the question arises whether it is possible to integrate and promote this ability within organizations. Various hypotheses can be formulated, but before doing that, lets explore some counterintuitive dynamics around learning, that ultimately affect its growth.

Learning is a natural process, inherent to organizational life. However, its impact is often implicit, regulating core processes. Regrettably, its own success may unsuspectingly trigger barriers to expand the capability to adapt.

These organizational hurdles primarily consist of restraints limiting the proper resourcing of learning units around the structure, *typically triggered when results are overly positive.* These cycles must be removed and replaced by reinforcing effects.

These *control effects* trigger a compensatory cycle, impairing primary learning. As growth and profits reach some thresholds, the incremental R&D value often comes into question. Divestiture in research is a sure way to boost short-term profits, *trading off vital, yet less visible long-term viability.*

The designer of learning organizations *should contemplate not only what to do, but also what not to do. Western incumbents face tremendous financial predictability pressure.* Their quarterly action-oriented nature can punish the balance of the learning system.

A diagram can help us visualize the challenges faced by managers, aiming to support learning, when navigating their organization's reinforcing cycles and compensatory processes.

QUATERLY PROGRESS BACKFIRING ON LEARNING

This isn't true for their Eastern counterparts, *who appear to succeed understanding the winner-takes-it-all nature of learning,* refraining from divesting in research when things go well.

Their actions exhibit a keen understanding of the impact of learning on their ecosystem[1], at all levels of the organization.

The result? The learning system becomes destabilized due to inadequate controls, and the instability intensifies as the level of 'short-term control' over the profit line increases.

The question then arises: How these structural barriers be eliminated? The answer lies in organizational design.

From setting up educational programs to selecting planning, incentives, and controls, every adjustment made by the designer has implications for the learning process.

However, we cannot undertake design by dealing with every parameter in isolation. The method needs to consider the entire system and the interactions between its components.

WE CAN ONLY DESIGN WHAT WE UNDERSTAND

'Every person can, if truly desires it, become the sculptor of his own brain' – RAMON Y CAJAL[2]

There is a significant gap in the study of Intelligent Organizations: *understanding how learning takes place and* depicting it on a *Representational Model,* to better understand the interactions between the key variables driving the process.

This representation will then assist the creation of solutions, resulting in a *Prescriptive Model.* Blueprints are adapted to maximize impact, given boundary constraints.

Then, we set the *Implementation Model,* where the emphasis at this point shifts from 'ends' to 'means': *how to best deploy and resource the new capabilities to augment learning.*

Finally, our proposal will focus on adapting proven methods to the realm of learning. It is critical to have a *Feedback Loop,* that enables periodic progress evaluations.

Herein, we introduce a staged design method for designing, establishing and maintaining learning organizations:

1) *Diagnosis with Precision:* The journey commences with setting up a *Representational Model.* This serves as an analytical assessment tailored for organizational learning. Leveraging artificial intelligence and microeconomic principles, it provides a comprehensive view of an organization's current learning standing and challenges.

2) *Designing with Insight:* Armed with clarity from the initial diagnosis, the focus shifts to the *Prescriptive Model.* This phase is about crafting bespoke solutions anchored in advanced cybernetic theories. It designs adapted blueprints to addresses specific learning challenges, laying the plan for organizational transformation.

3) *Execution with Confidence:* Culminating the process is the *Implementation Model.* Adapting proven methodologies, this phase operationalizes the insights from the preceding steps. It ensures the seamless integration of learning-centric changes into the organization's daily operations.

4) *Evaluate with Objectivity:* All of these three models should be constantly calibrated: *Is the learning quality the desired one? Are learning structures effective? Are all areas interacting synergistically to reinforce learning?*

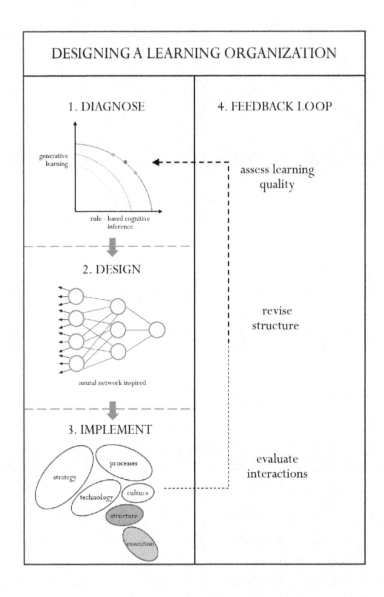

UNLOCKING THE POWER OF 'LEARNING BY DESIGN'

Our intention with the staged design method is to aim for a pragmatic framework, able to make the learning dimension tangible and help increase the adaptability of organizations.

Embracing each phase and tailoring it to specific organizational realities, should help pave the way for sustainable growth and industry leadership.

The outcome will be a staged design method for learning organizations, complete with diagnostic, prescriptive, and implementation models to assist the designer.

- *The Representational Model* will draw inspiration from a combination of AI and microeconomics paradigms, to document the problem constraints at hand.
- *The Prescriptive Framework* will get inspiration on recent progress in cybernetic theory for adaptive control of multi-variable nonlinear systems.
- *The Implementation Approach* will be method-agnostic, enabling designers to leverage existing methodologies, adding the dimensions required to maximize learning

***

The subsequent section will deep dive into visualization techniques, so as to be able to understand the nature of the creation exercise to be undertaken.

4

MODELLING LEARNING ORGANIZATIONS
A Renewal of Learning Paradigms

HOW CAN WE DEPICT a learning organization? This concern is more frequent among its members than many researchers might acknowledge.

The ability to accurately represent an organizational concept in a clear and concise manner that genuinely reflects the underlying learning process, can make the difference between a successfully implemented project and one relegated to the back of a filing cabinet.

The most successful representations today seem to lean in the representational language of the area of systems modelling. The graphical language of deterministic control systems captured the imagination of organizational scientists.

The successful dissemination of Forrester's system theory approach[1], further expanded by scholars like Senge, is largely attributable to the communicative power of its symbolic language. *Lean schematics are utilized to graphically explain the dynamics of systems with positive (destabilizing) and negative (stabilizing) feedback loops.* There is beauty in its simplicity:

SYSTEM THEORY: A VISUAL PROCESS LANGUAGE

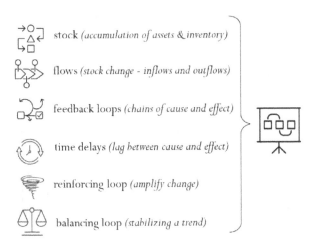

stock *(accumulation of assets & inventory)*

flows *(stock change - inflows and outflows)*

feedback loops *(chains of cause and effect)*

time delays *(lag between cause and effect)*

reinforcing loop *(amplify change)*

balancing loop *(stabilizing a trend)*

We propose that, similar to systems theory, organizational learning requires an array of visualization models:

- starting with visualizations to capture the components of *both 'generative' learning and 'reactive' learning*

- representations to demonstrate the skeleton supporting an organization's collective learning, and

- the components that support its ongoing operation

LEARNING ORGANIZATION MODELS:

THE GREAT VOID

Without diminishing the value of the contributions made in the field of organizational learning, a significant void remains: *no one, to our knowledge, has successfully represented the intrinsic learning processes of an organization and their supporting structures.*

In organizational theory, it is customary to represent organizational structures in diagrams, depicting reporting lines, with the resulting schematics *(organigrams)* proving invaluable to address span, functional scope, or layering issues.

TYPICAL ORGANIZATIONAL REPRESENTATIONS

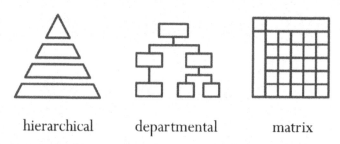

hierarchical   departmental   matrix

These representations allow organizational designers to depict reporting processes of highly hierarchical, functionally oriented, or matrix-oriented organizations. At a simple glance, managers can grasp the modifications in reporting relationships and bring to life the new structure, *typically setting processes around the defined power lines.*

Conveniently, the terminology used in organizational taxonomy - *hierarchical organizations, departmental constructs or matrix structures* - reflects the specific power paradigms that influenced the design, genesis, and growth of the organization.

However, the closer these diagrams get to represent learning is when depicting massive 'R & D', Strategic or Intelligence Organizations, like the WWII example below[2].

WWII INTELLIGENCE ORG CHART EXAMPLE

A magnificent chart of an organizational structure, so scaled, that its departments appear aligned against the core issues at the time, and even depicting some entities devoted to triaging or staging information across departments.

This is the closest we have seen a traditional org chart getting to represent learning structures, aligned with specific problems.

How important can a graphically representable model be?

Consider the value that Mintzberg's visualizations have provided to traditional organizational designers. These representations establish an organizational competence blueprint, whose appearance varies depending on type of organization, as to depict the size and arrangement of its components.

Visual models become not only a tool for designers, but a common language between them and organization members, representing a shared abstraction that will be put into practice when all desired elements are in place.

'To the thinking soul, images serve as if they were contents of perception' – ARISTOTLE[3]

However, for the Learning Organization designer, there seem to be no satisfactory tools available. Let's picture an academic or a consultant today, asked by a client to structurally enhance collective learning:

- *What model or methodology will they use?*

- *How can they graphically represent* the phenomenon of organizational learning?

- *How can they ensure that the model will effectively result* in an entity with improved learning?

- *What desired learning-related parameters* would result from specific structural modifications?

Exploring the absence of early learning organizational models, hypotheses generally fall into two categories:

- a perceived lack of interest or importance in the topic
- the presence of challenges in addressing the issue

The significant interest in organizational learning among academics and managers, along with the clear benefits that these models bring to organizational design, challenges the validity of the first hypothesis.

This suggests that the scarcity of models is not due to a lack of interest.

Consequently, it seems more plausible that the development of these models faced substantial obstacles from the onset, aligning with the second hypothesis.

EVOLUTION OF PARADIGMS IN LEARNING MODELS

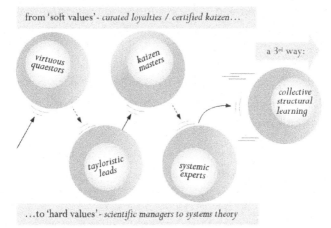

Unfortunately, we appear stuck in a cycle, *always empowering individuals either through hard or soft levers,* while *the collective learning process does not have a structural expression:*

Recurring Paradigm Shifts

The cycle appears triggered by organizations outgrowing their governance mechanisms, as progress kicks in:

1) The first strategic administrators are depicted in history as *'people of values;'* e.g., *Roman Quaestors (a renowned body of elite administrators)* following rigorous steps of a *cursus honorum,* to prove their competency and allegiance

2) The late XIX century left us an enduring legacy of *'enlightened individuals' leading learning;* such model falling prey to the realities of globalization post-WWII

3) Subsequently, *the focus shifted to sets of 'soft' policies or practices* aiming to influence decision-making mechanisms, typically involving more upward feedback *(e.g. Kaizen)*

4) More recently, *systems dynamics, brought back the promise of logical determinism,* with central modelling touted as team learning:

    -   *teams of specialists research in-depth complex problems and develop libraries of archetypes, or generalizations,* and

    -   *contradictorily, they dictate these representations back to the line,* akin to a sophisticated rule-based system

Let's review each one of these paradigms, *aiming to set the basis to find a 'third way' addressing the core issue: collective learning*

THE PARADIGM OF VIRTUOUS ADAPTATION:
THE SEARCH FOR A WISE MORAL GUARDIAN

The temptation to focus on individual learning, as an assured proxy to enhance organizational learning, may be the culprit.

Pre-Industrial Revolution organizations such as government, military, religious, agricultural or trade guilds would often look up *to an absolutist leader, or an empowered group of enlightened problem solvers, setting direction based on their analysis.* For every Pope, there was a Camarlengo; every Roman Emperor would have a Quaestor per province[4]...

Loyalties to a value system were paramount then, considered the primary attributes of performance. Stable systems for the most part, organizations kept contained to the scale of human cognition – for the most part designed in a way that, as a fractal, they would replicate another 'same size' operating unit, under the purview of a loyal, honorable administrator. *Innovations were few, learnt when performing the trade – often requiring a generational cycle.*

Defying the Renaissance, government, military corps, trading companies, continued operating under the same paradigm, well into the XIX century. Their expansion was often limited by the availability of these trusted administrators.

A notable exception: during the early 1800s, *technological military breakthroughs (artillery) created dismal differences in results.* Their value multiplied when deployed in an agile way in the field, calling for different operations. *Thus, the Napoleonic strategic system heralded the next paradigm: Scientific Management.*

47

THE PARADIGM OF RATIONAL THINKING:

SEEKING 221B, CORPORATE BAKER STREET

The Industrial Revolution increased complexity. Specialized companies emerged *(e.g., factories, shipping, railroads, banks)*. And Scientific Management, as formalized by Taylor[5], gave us the 'efficiency expert.'

At first sight, these efficiency experts were not dissimilar to their ancient *quaestor* version. *However, Tayloristic organizations clearly differentiated the management of field operations from strategy, research and process design activities.*

Regrettably, from the organizational learning perspective, this view continued to reinforce the paradigm of a few 'enlightened individuals', epitomizing learning, often seen as the result of a pure exercise in logic:

One individual 'expert lead' goes through all the processes of the enterprise, perusing efficiency gaps as a sort of corporate Sherlock Holmes, interpreting reality *(perceived as a set of objective and concrete facts)* in light of a formal body of logical operators based on a set of fundamental axioms.

The rational conclusions thus formed, and implemented decisions, become part of the relevant experience used in similar analyses in other situations, creating a theory along the way. *Under this paradigm learning is, more than anything, an exercise in applied logic by a talented few — projected onto the whole.*

'Insensibly one begins to twist facts to suit theories, instead of theories to suit facts' - SHERLOCK HOLMES (BY AC DOYLE)[6]

Schön expressed concern about the rational paradigm. Despite being a proponent of 'technical rationality,' he acknowledged the challenge of defining the problem itself. As he stated in *The Reflective Practitioner*[7], back in 1983:

> *'In the real world, problems do not present themselves as given. They must be constructed from fragments of situations that are confusing, challenging, uncertain. To turn a situation into a problem, a certain amount of work must be done: sense must be made of situations that initially lack it.'*

Back to the analogy of the great fictional detective *(which we use since it is based in a real-world scholar, Dr. Joseph Bell, a genius researcher, and professor of Sir Arthur Conan Doyle),* the 'method' would largely rely on evidence, to indeed define the problem:

- *Keen observation: unusual trends hold the most value*
- *Avoiding preconceptions:* 'park' existing theories
- *Gather facts:* needed to confirm possible solutions
- *Logical reasoning, hypothesis, generation, and testing*

In organizations, operational teams are often the first to stumble upon new pieces of 'evidence' *showing that a 'theory in use', as Argyris termed it, is losing its validity and needs adaptation.*

However, the complexity of human communication *(affected by competition and collaboration)* hampers clarity in large set ups. Delayed, distorted messages handicap the ability of *scientific managers* to respond. *Maybe time to abdicate centralization and shift focus back to distributed values...*

THE PARADIGM OF HOLISTIC LEARNING:

BACK TO THE APPEALS OF THE VALUE SYSTEM

A major challenge coming into play was the limitation of our own individual rational inference. If it is hard to explain the individual learning experience of an expert, just imagine trying to map out the collective interaction of thousands of individuals.

The sheer scale reached by Industrial Revolution behemoths in the Post War, imposed further separations between *execution and design, operations and strategy.* The *'talented few'* heroes of the past, *could quickly become a liability,* drafting strategy confined in *'ivory towers,'* unaware of *(or unable to process)* the competitive needs of global playing fields.

This empowered the emergence of a fatalistic view, in which tracking granular facts systematically, across vast industrial complexes, was deemed to be unrealistic.

> However, a quick-fix could be of order: *addressing the divide built over the years of separation between shop floors and engineering.*
> Oversimplifying the Japanese examples discussed, their *Kaizen-type*[8] methods *created immense value by improving problem-framing through better data collection.*

Organizational learning shifted then, to be considered more of an art than a science and soon became in itself a bestseller's buzzword. The term is fresh, innovative, and appealing: the fashionable thing is to become a *'learning leader'* who improves through communications the *'IQ'* of their organizations.

THE PARADIGM OF SYSTEMIC ADAPTATION:

SWINGING BACK TO DETERMINISTIC MODELLING

It is painful to acknowledge the unintended paralyzing implications of the 'holistic learning' approaches. While other scientific disciplines will continue to plow through the understanding of complex systems, management theorists seemed contempt to just tout the benefits of flatter, more transparent organizations.

In doing so, they somewhat ignored the realities of time lags, budgeting constraints and non-linearities – as well as the abundant conflicts of interest and selfish behavior of rational individual actors. While the approach would add value to an extent, it would discourage further exploration into the fabric of collective interaction and learning.

And, to the surprise of many, an unsuspecting scientific discipline claimed turf into advancing the organizational learning cause: *Systems Theory*

Mathematical models, fueled by transactional data, could shed light at scale across some problems humans would find very hard to act upon. Incentives would often refrain the unfettered truth to be put forward, and short-term focus would focus organizations into *'linear symptoms' as opposed to 'non-linear causes.'*

However, there is more than math to them: an attractive and appealing visual language: *Simple diagrams of processes, supplemented with feedback loops to represent compensatory variables, becoming easier to simulate their behavior in a computer.*[9]

Dynamic systems aim to make the concept of causality clear and accessible to all members of an organization. Building the model is a laborious process, involving the inclusion of a large number of dozens or even hundreds, of variables.

By running simulations on a computer, we show managers how their assumptions and actions might not always achieve the desired outcomes. *The model is ultimately used to design policies, which underpin the rules for the decision-making system.*

Why would the area of dynamic systems somehow bring the rational inference paradigm back into the picture?

> *The key consideration is about the creators of the model.* Complex models need specialists who can identify key variables, analyze how they interact, and understand the system's feedback mechanisms.

Isn't this effort then promoting the return of the centralized *'enlightened efficiency expert'* within the organization?

- The process of constructing the model, is typically carried out by specialists external to the unit/organization

- The resulting model, albeit a fact-based solution, is the work of a few, for a while, and not the collective

- The solution to the bounded problem is given then to execution teams: 'hard' definitions based on data

- *Learning as a two-stage process*: a generative phase *(model development), followed by a reactive period, deployment*

To analyze this proposition, it is helpful to consider the perspective of Jay Forrester, *the founder of the field of dynamic systems,* on how these systems should be conceived and applied. As he wrote in his book, *Industrial Dynamics*[1]:

'*Conventional methods for designing organizations simply cannot cope with dynamic complexity. In mathematical terms, the task of constructing organizations that function in the real world is far more complex than solving a nonlinear, tenth-order differential equation. No engineer or mathematician can solve such a system through intuition and debate alone. It is unreasonable to expect managers to be able to do so...*'

A major paradox is that a few external individuals often carry the burden of generative learning. This approach may limit the overall learning capability of the organization.

Imagine a second stage of spreading information:

'*Teams, these are your processes. Familiarize yourself with them, look at this diagram explaining some of the counterintuitive interrelationships between the basic variables, do not worry about inconsistencies of the reports yielded upwards. After all, you only have a partial view of the system.*'

Learning from here on is essentially reactive. Managers interact with the new model, an *ad hoc* paradigm created for their teams, implementing it as a new, rule-based system.

Once more, organizational learning theory gets stuck in the 'hard' rationality approach, creating tension with the 'soft' values approach. Has anyone heard about *Six Sigma* yet?

ORGANIZATIONAL LEARNING CROSSROADS

This strong position depicts the crossroads currently encountered in the field of Organizational Learning:

1) *Be absorbed as a hard discipline within Dynamic Modeling,* almost manifesting *as an 'intelligent design' discipline:*

   - *Collective learning appears performed by skilled corporate strategy or consulting teams (i.e., not an inherent capability close to the operational structure)*

   - *Occurs mostly at specific crisis points in space and time,* leaving a new legacy or paradigm, which in turn will be the subject of reactive learning

   - *Self-assessment of learning processes is rarely in scope,* the objective *is to gather information about core processes,* enhancing decisions around them

2) *Cultivate Systems Thinking as a soft practice,* across the organization, *hoping to spark an evolutionary approach:*

   - *Team learning happens by enabling core operational team members* and creating a *kaizen-style* charter, encouraging them to creatively explore ideas

   - *Learning through practice, the perspective is internal and 'bottoms up':* 'How can to cultivate attitudes that allow more learning, and sharing?

   - Organizational learning is, in essence, *still individual-centric*, and systemic models are means, not ends, to catalyze this process

SEEKING A THIRD OPTION:

CAN WE EMBRACE DESIGN TO FOSTER COLLECTIVE LEARNING?

In the previous section, two possible paths for the discipline of Organizational Learning were deliberately presented in the form of exclusive alternatives.

Both have one thing in common *(regrettably a weakness)*: They envision Organizational Learning *in ways that the very structure of the learning organization takes a back seat.*

However, in this section, it is proposed that these alternatives are not mutually exclusive. They are options that should coexist and interact, bundled together by an, until now, elusive fabric of collective learning.

The Creation of a Structural Learning Paradigm

The new paradigm is based on a simple principle: *Collective learning happens on the interaction network,* the communication array between the information processing entities *(whatever they composition or capability).*

Bottoms-up insights (not just raw data) flow through the network, from the operational core functions upwards, triggering actions within the realm of their processing capacity *(people, processes, and systems).*

Strategic, top-down actions, focus primarily in honing these learning networks – acting directly only in contingency cases.

Much like a biological brain *processes external stimuli, interpreting reality and triggering unconscious or conscious actions,* we will explore organizational learning that results from layers of 'processors' in the organization. *These analyze features, known or unknown, and execute or route new analyses accordingly.*

For simplicity, we can visualize two types of learning layers, one assisting core 'motor' processes, and a higher level one ensuring overall learning adequacy, resiliency, and planning:

- *parasystemic learning:* distributed across the organization and running parallel to all the core operating units *(hence their name, learning from them and with them, as an established capability),* and
- *metasystemic learning:* interconnected centrally across all the organization, measuring the performance of each learning parasystem and assessing future needs

---

Differently to prior paradigms, in the proposed approach, *rationality or values are not alternatives, just concurrent features of the networked learning system.* Operators, experts, models, set processes – all are part of an interconnected learning web that we can model, plan, and represent.

New systems, storage and communications enable levels of interconnection that were not possible before. The current Information Revolution brings with it powerful frameworks both to enhance and to understand collective learning.

For these learning networks to operate optimally, we need to understand how to set them up to:

- Enhance their feature extraction capabilities and problem identification – as Schön would suggest
- Model complex scenarios effectively, as advocated by Forrester, and
- Improve communication, both vertically and laterally, as recommended by Deming, or even Cicero[10].

More importantly, as we can leverage novel building blocks like electronic communications, relational data storage, and individual computing power, *we are well equipped to explore the nature of collective learning with powerful new frameworks.*

In doing so, especially in the field of organizational sciences, we might realize that we've been focusing too much on the trees and missing the forest. Ahead of us lies a rich ecosystem, which we can better understand by stepping back and looking at its overarching structures, its 'canopies'.

***

We will focus next on the nature of Learning Parasystems, the foundational layer supporting core processes.

5

———

PARASYSTEMS:
THE FOUNDATION

Connecting the Neurons...

O RGANIZATIONS ARE INDEED ABLE TO LEARN. Undoubtedly, organizational learning is closely connected to the learning of its members, analogous to how our individual, cerebral, learning capacity is related to the learning of our neurons. The aim of this section is to delve into the notion of organizational learning systems as meta-systems that process information in a distributed, parallel, and extensive manner.

In such a system, the ability to learn and transform information into knowledge is not derived from a rational process, but through a procedure we refer to as 'neural.' *The learning capacity is determined by the structural arrangement of the collective system's information-processing elements.* This new structural learning paradigm will allow the adoption of a network model that explicitly makes the design of an organization's learning system accessible.

ORGANIZATIONAL LEARNING PARASYSTEMS

WORKING IN PARALLEL TO ENHANCE CORE PROCESSES

The first step to understanding the collective learning concepts expressed here and the designability of these characteristics in organizations is to comprehend the parasystemic nature of reactive learning associated with organizational processes. To do this, the following 'textbook' visualization exercise may be helpful:

CORE ORGANIZATIONAL PROCESS FLOW

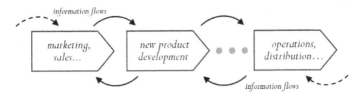

Let us begin with the view of an organization as a chain of interacting processes. Different representations can support this vision: sequences of boxes or arrows, representing different interconnected processes consecutively, *Porterian* value chains[1], or loops in the style of *The Fifth Discipline*[2], which seek to capture systemic relationships among processes.

What is essential for us is that these processes are primarily sequences of activities *(which we will call procedures)*, where the *illusion of linearity* is given by chaining them.

The idea in traditional organizational design is to represent the existence of harmonious interaction among primary and support units, without exposing the details of their information exchanges.

THE COORDINATION ILLUSION:
PRIMARY AND SUPPORT UNITS 'IN TUNE'

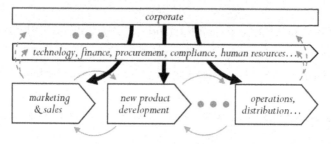

However, even the more detailed frameworks, depicting layers of common services across the business value chain, fail to illustrate how decision makers perform informed choices.

Information may be more or less relevant to the next process partner, and key analysis require support from, *often scarce,* expert units.

Procedures can differ greatly depending on the nature of the process. In some cases, inputs must be transformed using specialized machinery *(manufacturing),* while in others, they are simply accounted for *(warehousing).*

Some activities may not even be performed by the entity, being outsourced and subject to lax control by it. *But they all have one thing in common: they require and generate information.*

REALITY: AD HOC, UNPLANNED, POLITICIZED
INFORMATION EXCHANGES

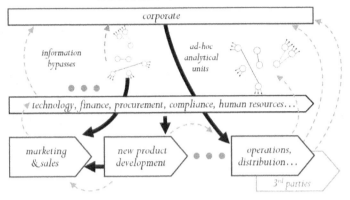

Just like a free market adapts to changes in demand and supply, a unit naturally tries to adapt to its changing knowledge needs, mostly fueled by its own team member's incentives.

Individuals would gravitate towards learning what they deem most needed or valuable at the time, perhaps without consciously intending to fulfill collective learning needs.

But, how to understand what information is processed, by whom? What decisions are taken? Who evaluates the outcomes? The task is daunting when looking at the whole organizational construct.

DECODING UNIT LEARNING

'Adult nerves appear fixed and immutable... but not in the embryonic tissues'- RAMON Y CAJAL[3]

The great Spanish scientist succeeded, where others had failed, by searching for the first brain cell by looking at the simplest organism: *a chicken embryo, within a humble farm egg.*

Similarly, to decode organizational learning, we must look first at basic core operational units and understand their information flows. By applying that angle, *we realize that core units communicate primarily operational data, typically in a straightforward sequential fashion.*

INSTINCTUAL PROCESSING: THE AMPHIBIAN BRAIN

They assess the situation, react, and provide minimal data for the next step. They typically *report other aggregated metrics upstream upon acting.* In most cases, the upstream reporting just registers execution pace. Think of a field sales team, just dishing out more proposals to 'easier targets', avoiding risks...

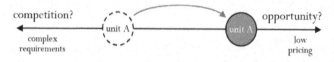

LEAPING FROM DESCRIPTION TO ACTION

However, in other cases, information reported upstream *can trigger a pause to reassess targets and actions.* In this case, *there is an outcome,* an assessment, reflecting about new options needed.

ANALYTICAL PROCESSING: THE MAMMALIAN BRAIN

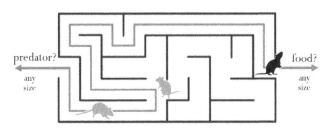

The unit's data can be classified according to its purpose:

1) *Descriptive,* qualifying the input attributes to trigger actions. *Oriented to in-process routine services (what to do)*

2) *Operational,* necessary to execute each of the tasks *(focused on actions, how to do),* and

3) *Qualitative,* providing information on the efficiency of the processes *(comparing results with the objective)*

ELEVATING FROM PRACTICE TO LEADERSHIP

The key questions to address are:

- *Who manages these information flows, if anyone?*
- *How is data collected, processed, and interpreted?*

These decisions are made by systems adjacent to the process, sometimes external to the unit, acting de facto as parasystems.

PARASYSTEMS:

THE 'INVISIBLE LEARNING HAND'

What is a parasystem? Think about *an adjacent, parallel system,* sort of a transducer feeding from data supplied by the tasks, which in turn, provides information required by the processes.

LEARNING PARASYSTEMS

At first glance, the defined parasystem must perform at least two essential functions:

- Firstly, it carries out **core perceptive** *or sensory* activities that evaluate the information processing

- Secondly, it performs *(contingent)* **motor** *or command* functions, which provides the underlying process with required input to address complex or novel situations
- Third, **reports on the unit's combined learning effectiveness** to higher control centers

These commands effectively regulate the adaptability of the process, and their complexity depends on the stability of the controlled system when facing a changing environment.

At times, they intervene by compensating not only for *'operational variables'* but also for *'design variables'* of the tasks involved in the corresponding procedure *(typically minor adjustments at this level, depending on empowerment provided).*

CORE SYSTEMS AND LEARNING PARASYSTEMS

core systems

parasystems

sense
decide
schedule
fulfill
record

unit
learning

verify
analyze
compare
suggest
fix

To make it clearer: If external information could *always* be directly converted into successful action commands by the operational unit, *a learning parasystem would not be necessary.*

The parasystems act in parallel, as their name suggests, tracking both the correctness of the decisions taken *(consistency)* and the degree of success of their output *(effectiveness),* independently.

It is by merit of that proximity to the process, yet acting in an exempt manner, that they can both

a) Help address immediate, novel situations, and
b) More importantly, *interpret* what is needed to evolve the subject system over time.

This point is crucial: *what does it mean to interpret?* To interpret is to understand and convey the meaning of something.

The parasystem must be able to relate input variables *(type 1, descriptive information)* from many sources *(core operational units, market, shared service units)* and supply an assessment on the impact on the output variables *(type 2, operational information).*

As we have discussed, learning is not complete without a self-critical results evaluation. In neurological systems, feedback assimilation alters the processing patterns, enhancing response for future actions.

Once the *action-evaluation* cycle occurs, *'type 3 data'* comes into play, *indicating the level of satisfaction against the desired target.* This data *(bearing information about learning quality)* is then fed back into the systems and associated parasystems, with varying degrees of granularity, intensity, and time delay.

The obtained results are constantly compared to the desired ones. What is the purpose of this monitoring? To compensate and adjust the interpretative process related to the underlying operational procedures to reduce the difference between expected and obtained values.

And this is simply learning, in a way that enables further adaptation improvements. The described parasystemic structure is a critical component of learning. Data acquisition, processing, and transmission of information occur in a cycle where the level of adjustment should be commensurate to the gap between obtained results and desired parameters.

Understanding and addressing this gap is key to enabling the acceleration of learning.

REPRESENTING TYPES OF LEARNING

What type of learning occurs in the parasystem? It could involve a mix of both *reactive, inference-based deductions* from past rules, and *generative learning,* capable of addressing new situations.

As the parasystem learns, it determines how best to adapt to the future by assessing our current decision-making processes. It aims to solve operational problems more effectively than competitors within the procedure's scope.

The results of this process are most evident when the output feedback matrix is applied to the system, leading to:

- *Modification in operational sequences,*
- *Creation of new features or process steps, and*
- *Elimination of tasks, that are either outdated or redundant*

However, it is important to note that every situation may require different learning types, awareness, and intensity. Let's characterize two extreme types:

1. *Rule-based cognitive inference:* the most prevalent learning type. *Usually, under normal operations,* the system reacts primarily by deploying frameworks set by previous actions

   - *The frequency of the problem* is often associated with its immediate solvability: *the most frequent and well-known problems are acted upon by applying pre-established routines*

   - *Their resolution depends primarily on rules or accepted interpretations set in memory:* the routine used successfully in previous instances is automatically triggered once the input variable pattern is identified

   - *The speed of producing an appropriate response* depends on the direct applicability of the stored 'recipe,' the ease of accessing the 'file' of successful routines, and the integrity with which they have been preserved

   - *Simple or complex problems may fit this framework.* As far as the problem frequency is there, it is highly likely the organization has generated documented ways to respond to it *(regardless of its efficiency or efficacy)*

2. *Generative learning: On the other hand, completely new problems receive different treatment.*
   - Unlike repeated problems, the situations may just start to occur or be large, *'one-in-a-lifetime'* events. Its

historical frequency may be lower, but either their impact or growth rate causes the need to react

- This learning type *depends primarily on the hypotheses-generation capacity of the parasystem, and its ability to trigger experimentation,* jointly with the operational unit

- The parasystem must generate and test options until it achieves an understanding of the input pattern and its relationship with output variables. *Through ideation, simulation and trial-and-error, a solution is outlined*

- These can in turn evolve into a new research capability or even a set of new routines, blending then over time with rule-based inferencing

So, both types of learning can *blend (more often than not they do),* and different units in the organization may have their own mix in terms of learning style.

Also, both learning modalities have a few things in common: if the situation never repeats, the associated systems and parasystems will gradually forget what they learned.

In some cases, it could be said that recent learnings could just linger for a while in short-term memory and never transfer to long-term memory. *Only sheer impact, or frequency of problem repetition, refines and reaffirms the solution sets in memory.*

In Artificial Intelligence (AI) literature, these two learning modalities are known as two classical paradigms: *rule-based systems and generate-and-test systems.*

Interestingly, of all the learning paradigms used in AI, these two have been the most successful:

- *Rule-based systems,* leveraging inference and logical rules have been the foundation of expert systems, coded in AI specific languages such as LISP and Prolog. Also optimization algorithms belong in this category.

- *Generate-and-test systems* are mostly enabled by a newer computational discipline, neural networks, some of which have the capability to self-organize and seek conversion by generating random scenarios.

It might be tempting to use the AI models corresponding to each of these paradigms to classify various learning parasystems across a given organizational structure.

However, it is not a straightforward exercise, since organizational learning, even at this initial level being analyzed, exhibits mixed behavior, blending almost invariably, to some degrees rule-based and generative paradigms.

An appropriate diagnostic model should be capable of portraying these intermediate situations.

Graphically, one could visualize a two-dimensional 'learning supply' space:

The vertical axis represents the system's generation and testing capacity, while the horizontal axis displays its ability to adapt through rule-based solutions.

VISUALIZING THE 'LEARNING SUPPLY' SPACE

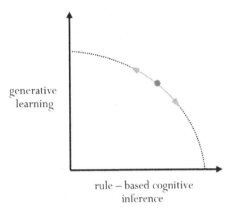

generative
learning

rule – based cognitive
inference

In new situations where stored knowledge is less relevant, high-performing companies or internal units appear to behave more like a *generate-and-test system, closer to the vertical axis.*

Conversely, the horizontal axis depicts learning set-ups optimized around rules, typically effective when dealing with high frequency, similar type of issues. These systems shift towards efficient rule-based systems and protocols, *favoring incremental learning, evolving gradually from a cumulative knowledge base.*

As an example, an airline 'ground' airport team may be enabled by parasystems to solve complex recurring problems in a very systematic manner *(such as relocating people after an overnight flight cancellation).*

The same airline may have their financial team, dealing with problems that require a more fluid approach, such as an oil crisis that sends the fuel cost skyrocketing, boiling down options ranging from *financial hedging, investor relations communications, cost cutting, repricing — or all of the above.*

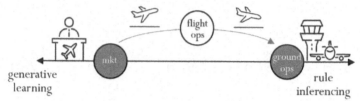

generative
learning

rule
inferencing

AIRLINE EXAMPLE: FUNCTIONS LEARN DIFFERENTLY

Thus, the framework allows to depict the required learning mix, which usually follows the nature of the problem set *(not the other way around).*

In our airline example, there will be airlines much better equipped to deal with fuel price changes than others, and those reputed for having flawless logistics on the ground.

However, it is not only about the 'learning mix': superior learners create more competitive environments, challenging their peers, creating a need for 'more learning' capacity; *more IQ...*

REPRESENTING INTENSITY OF LEARNING

Let's imagine that any point in that curve illustrates a function where regardless of the mix of different learning types *(i.e., more adaptive or rule based),* the overall adaptation capacity of the organization along that curve is constant.

ORGANIZATIONAL LEARNING ISOQUANTS

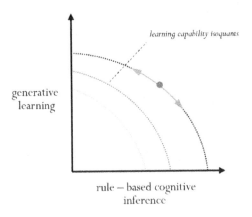

We can visualize this space partitionable by learning 'isoquants'.

These are parallel lines illustrating *equivalent learning capacity along the same mix profile* (hence the name '*iso*', *equal* and '*quant*', *quantity*) each one of them characterizing equal levels of problem solving, independently from the learning mix.

The further away from the origin, the larger the learning capacity.

The pair of Cartesian axes thus defines a vector space in *which:*

- *Its angular orientation* expresses its generation capacity relative to its rule inference capacity, and

- *The vector's magnitude represents a particular parasystem's learning capacity*

PARASISTEMIC LEARNING PROFILES

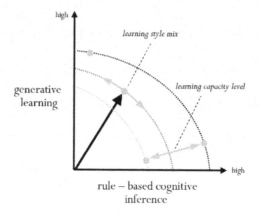

rule – based cognitive
inference

The learning space thus defined becomes *an initial diagnosis visualization framework,* able to depict different situations:

-   Parasystems vectors angles reflect mix *(e.g., new unit in a new market or established one in a stagnant one)*

-   *Alternative, units with similar profile in terms of* mix, will reach different isoquants based on capacity.

Let's see how this would work in practice.

Let's imagine a small copier shop, like one of those that every college campus has, or the one in your neighborhood.

Let's say call this small copy shop 'x'.

Upon examination of its core processes and supporting parasystems, 'x' potentially would depict *a somewhat structured, non-intense learning profile:*

SMALL COPY SERVICES SHOP

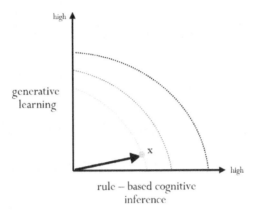

- Jobs get in, *a menu of limited pricing options is configured based on urgency,* deadlines for each work order get established

- Employees are trained to conduct repetitive tasks, inclusive of copier's issues *(all copiers are the same model),* and

- Schedules and production incentives are set

The rationale is straight forward: at the end, in an stable environment, this case is typical of companies that has a very low need to solve for complex problems:

- 'Type 1' information *(work orders)* are almost perfectly matched by 'type 2' output, *(schedule instructions)* supporting execution

- Workload adjustments are routine, equipment failures have a set procedure, *within certain thresholds of capacity*

In this scenario, 'type 3' information *(feedback)* is rare to happen, since typically there are few gaps between demand and results, *on a commodity, predictable service*

> *However, a lost original, a late job, three sick team members not showing to work, an unexplained demand surged... any one of those events will trigger a change in the learning profile*

This may take the form of a temporary crisis, *resulting in an increased learning capacity of the team* on an ongoing basis.

Staff training, 'one off' equipment adds, early morning checks on staff during critical days to ensure capacity, all of these are collective learnings, either documented somewhere or in the head of the shop owner and managers.

This last distinction is important. The resulting learning mix after this crisis can be different, either through refined procedures *(reinforcing rules)* or more experienced managers able to make decisions on the fly.

Now let's picture a major copy shop chain, 'Big X,' basically the same business model, but across multiple locations:

- As far as 'Big X' has the same services, they may have a similar learning profile to the small copy shop 'x'

- *That said, they operate in different markets, exposed to more client types, and have multiple high-capacity copier brands.*

LARGE COPY SERVICES SHOP

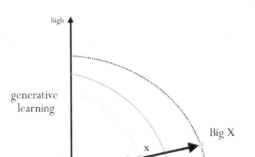

All things being equal, it would be fair to assume that 'Big X' just learns more, their processes are better structured.

In real life, closer looks would surface that they do a few other things too — *however their intrinsic learning systems support a repetitive operational business, ideally suited for rule-based learning.*

For instance, 'Big X' probably process larger amounts of 'type 3' information, feedback, at scale and they also have some other problems to address: *brand building, payroll, business planning.*

However, to characterize a very different profile, in the same sector.

Let's meet company 'c', serving all your printing and copying needs, at their first location in a brand-new office building:

'PRINT AND COPY' SERVICES SHOP

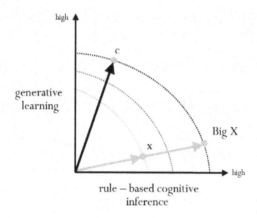

Interestingly, company 'c' is small too, maybe even smaller than company 'x', a thriving established business on campus.

But company 'c' leadership saw a market opportunity: They bought new Cannon multifunction machines that can both print and copy and they are running a pilot to prove the model.

They connect to the Local Area Network (LANs) of the different offices and offer them the entire outsourcing of their printing, copy and fax rooms.

Some of their processes are actually simpler: customers rarely show up for print jobs, they do that from PCs upstairs, but other issues are nightmarish… connecting to networks, collating unplanned printouts on the floor, tracking a printout that is actually a fax, and rushing the confirmation upstairs.

> *So, this is a very promising business — if they survive their trove of operational problems, as they catch up with the learning curve.*
>
> *A small part of their business is commoditized (some clients do show up downstairs to just copy something), but largely they run a networking operation, connected to demanding clients with different IT standards and business needs.*

The organization is in constant 'generative mode', processing a lot of feedback about new problems and reconfiguring units, thinking 'out of the box:

- salespeople are critical, and they need to understand networking, *a precondition for clients to operate with 'c'*
- traditional 'copy shop' operators need to be retrained in the new technology and functions, and
- the initial Canon models purchased are not high-volume equipment, maybe they should install high throughput models for the larger clients in their own floors...

MAPPING OUT PARASYSTEMIC LEARNING

CROSS INDUSTRY EXAMPLES

Let's reflect into the key attributes of learning parasystems supporting successful organizations across different industries:

'Risk & profit' *(Venture Capital Analysis Unit):* Several investment banks are setting up new Venture Capital funds.

In doing so, they create units whose 'processes' consist of analyzing business, mainly to determine its chances of success and issuing investment opinions:

- *The nature of the prospect candidates is very diverse,* and projects rarely repeat, seeking new market opportunities
- *Analyzing non-existent / novel markets* involves working with little history to rely upon, mostly trending data
- Evidently, *rules or routines play less of a role here*
- Every case is new and constitutes a test. Moreover, data about business success may need to wait a couple of years

'Consulting & co' *(Consulting Firm):* A consulting team working on a difficult problem for a client has a very clear learning and situation analysis process, culminating in the elaboration of a report with strategic recommendations:

- The process is primarily generative, proposing and discarding ideas, however
- Depending upon the area there may be frameworks with some golden rules to accelerate analysis
- Hence, consultancies emphasize not only know-how generation but preserving it for the future

'Creads' *(Marketing Unit for a Mass Consumer Product):* The process performed by these units at large companies follows a well-honed playbook *(research, consumer cycles, media adds),* yet needing to incorporate creative agencies and respond to crisis:

- Monitor the market, detect consumer response changes, and apply actions *(promotions, advertising campaigns, etc.)*

- Companies like Heinz, Procter & Gamble have immense experience *(stored as segment knowledge)* managing brands
- Maneuvers such as relaunching products with 'improved formulas', special offers, and contests to engage the public
- However, not all their problems solved by applying norms:

  ..Emergencies do occur *(e.g., Tylenol Recall in 1982)*

  Brands displacing entry segment (e.g. Old Spice case study)

'Townburger' *(Fast Food Restaurant Production Unit):* The kitchen of a fast-food restaurant *(like McDonalds or Burger King)* has a well-defined process by design:

- Ingredients arrive to the restaurants in standardized formats, as do production orders
- Customers have just a few customization options
- Fast-food franchisees often consist of the use of the brand, corporate supervision, and *a comprehensive book of procedures detailing all aspects of the business*

So in some cases, *generative learning is of order,* the imperative is to craft units able to swiftly tackle novel problems and generate ad-hoc, custom responses.

In others, *successful problem-solving requires operating from rules,* keeping the generation of alternatives to a minimum.

'We're not in the hamburger business. We're in show business'— RAY KROK[4]

Our graphic framework represent the learning profiles just discussed. However, these can differ for players within an industry, teams within a company, or evolve over time.

PARASYSTEMIC LEARNING EXAMPLES

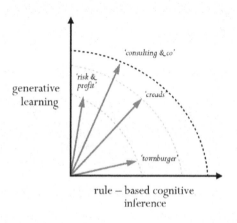

Ray Krok, the legendary McDonald's CEO would agree with a kitchen being organized, *yet for him, McDonald's was akin to Disney: An experience.*

Welcome to the Happy Meal concept, a generative unit within a structured business.

The learning mix depends on the problem statement definition, and whether the aim in a specific area is to thrive or just survive.

WHAT TYPE OF LEARNING IS NEEDED?
IT DEPENDS...

Let's discuss now the 'demand side' of learning, key to anchor the learning type bound to succeed in each situation.

CHALLENGES TO ADDRESS

	SIMPLE, STABLE	COMPLEX, ADAPTIVE
FREQUENT	routine challenges	strategic imperatives
OCCASIONAL	minor issues	sporadic crisis

When discussing the learning types, *their assessed success would depend primarily in meeting the demand pattern, in terms of:*

- Complexity, *referring to the number of variables in play, constraints (e.g., time, resources) and nonlinear cause-effects*
- Frequency, *related with the occurrence in volume terms, percent of total, seasonality, trend growth and predictability*

Similarly to the 'learning offer' space, there is a 'challenge demand' space.

In this case, the vertical axis represents the *frequency of the problems (let's think for simplicity that we focus just on occurrence rate)*, and the vertical axis their complexity and variability profile, also simplifying multi-dimensional attributes.

PARASISTEMIC LEARNING PROFILES

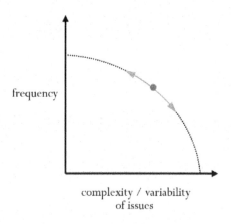

complexity / variability
of issues

Below, *a few examples the 'challenge curve'* can represent:

- *Minor issues:* an *ad-hoc, uncommon single* customer mishap

- *Routine challenges: weather-related, industry cycle events*

- *Sporadic challenges:* insider, outsider threat to a brand

- *Strategic imperatives:* a new, unexpected disruptive technology emerged on the horizon. *Innovate or die.*

And of course the intensity of the problems can differ widely.

-A sporadic problem with one customer can be critical, *if you run a Michelin-rated restaurant, and that customer is a celebrity*

-Or a major tech disruption may be easy to solve by severing the *gordian knot:* quit the business altogether and refocus energy in your strongholds, not yet under attack

PROBLEMS CHANGE THROUGH TIME

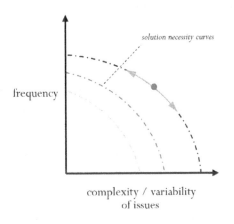

Isoquants here depict problem intensity. They evolve through time, sometimes featuring major disruptions.

A good example is the irruption of Computer Numeric Control in the textile industry.

Manual weaving gave in to cheap, low quality, punched cards machinery (Jacquard, 1804). Computers in the 1970s allowed for the automation of complex, varying patterns exceeding all cost and quality benchmarks. Time for reinvention.

WHAT TYPE OF LEARNING IS NEEDED, AGAIN?

LET'S MATCH LEARNING'S SUPPLY AND DEMAND...

To seek the optimal learning type, let's find 'learning equilibrium':

'TRANSPOSING' THE DEMAND SPACE...

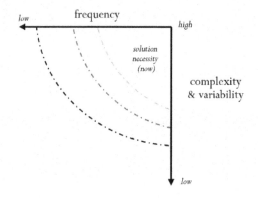

...LET'S BRING IN LEARNING SUPPLY

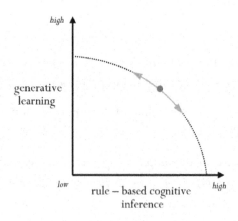

The next step will seek the intersection of demand and supply.

'I'm famous for saying 'it depends', I don't believe there are simple answers to economic questions' – *MILTON FRIEDMAN*[5]

So, inspired by Marshal's[6] work, *the first economist to fit curves of supply and demand for goods,* we can match our *defined learning and challenge curves, which requires reversing the challenge space scales:*

MATCHING LEARNING AND CHALLENGE SPACES

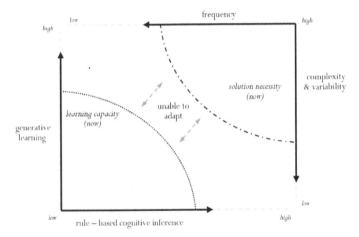

In the challenge space so defined, *the superior righthand corner corresponds to the toughest, higher frequency problems,* only matched by superior learning levels.

If the learning capacity curve cannot expand in a way that is able to intercept the challenge curve, there is a 'learning gap' state, in our opinion the most dangerous situation a company can be: *The larger the gap, the faster competitiveness is lost.*

'Data! Data! Data! I can't make bricks without clay. The game is on, Watson' — *SHERLOCK HOLMES (SIR A.C. DOYLE)* [7]

The game is on: **reaching the optimal learning point.** Any learning gaps must be addressed asap. *Like detective work, sources of inefficiency, competitive pressure, everything needs to be assessed.*

OPTIMAL LEARNING POINT

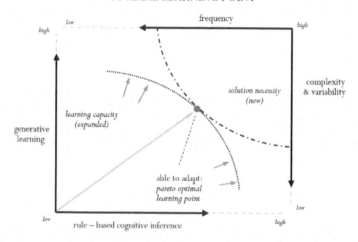

The *'Optimal Learning Point'* occurs when the learning curve and challenge curves touch each other, tangentially.

At this junction, the collective organization has the learning capacity required to match the problems. Two critical items:

a) *The right mix of learning types,* to reach the challenge space

b) *Monitor the situation, any larger challenge will result in a gap*

So, the ideal will be to create a buffer zone. *By placing more intensity in the system and understanding the potential shapes of the curves, these will intersect in multiple points of this space,* creating a range of options to solve problems.

The result is a *'buffered learning space'*, offering some leeway in terms of choosing learning styles or facing future change.

BUFFERED LEARNING SPACE

'Can one desire too much of a good thing' — SHAKESPEARE

The ideal scenario of creating a massive buffer space is a compelling idea to create competitive advantage, and sometime companies are tempted by in. However:

- Overproducing learning *is costly,* avoid *undue overflows*
- It may get in the way *of consistent learning methods*

The Microeconomics of Parasystems

Recapping on the framework, it contributes to clarify the goal, *although we have been considering only static situations so far:*

- *Learning Supply and Challenge Demand Analysis:* how the two curves interact to determine the *Optimal Learning Point* for a parasystem

However, if there are existing *(or foreseeable)* learning gaps, it is paramount to understand how to best shape the learning supply curves *(elasticity),* what effort *(cost)* is required to increase learning capacity, *and what is the cost of those desirable 'learning buffers' — i.e. can we afford them.*

- *Concept of Elasticity:* how much the supply of learning, quantitatively, responds to investment. This concept is fundamental in understanding learning *'plasticity'*
- *Costs and Production:* relationship between costs and production, particularly the ideas of increasing and diminishing returns
- *Marginal Learning Utility:* the value of a learning investment should be set by its estimated benefit

These last concepts are key for optimization, from a Pareto[8] standpoint: *elasticity, cost and marginal utility.*

Pareto's law of the vital few, or the 80/20 rule, states that for many events, roughly 80% of the effects come from 20% of the causes.

In Search of the Law of the 'Learning Vital Few':
Time and Cost

To continue from this point on, we need to pause and reflect *on the multi-variate nature of the problem* we are trying to solve:

1) *The 'challenge demand' curve moves through time* – typically in some shape or form towards the superior right hand corner. *And the learning offer curves must follow:*

   - *If commoditization, appearance of a substitute product or regulation* slows down progress, *the curves could 'ease'*

   - Otherwise, more commonly, *technological advances force a winner-takes-it-all dynamic*, where player's ability to timely increase learning is key to succeed

2) *The cost of the factors to produce learning will vary* depending on many other variables. Among others:
   - *The degree of skill level needed to produce impact (human experts, systems, or process expertise)*, more expensive to source, the higher the level of performance is…
   - *The competitive intensity in some areas to source those skills*
   - *The shape of the supply curve*, reflective of the elasticity of learning factors *(e.g. how easy or difficult are to inject those into an organization, with differing cost for learning type..*

So, *reaching for the optimal learning point in the most efficient manner* is both a problem that depends on how the target *(challenge demand)* is moving through time, and also the constraints placed by the interchange costs implied in the isoquant sets, and the relative costs of the factors available to increase each type of learning.

Fortunately, Francis Ysidro Edgeworth[9] worked on a similar mathematical problem and rendered us a framework that can be adapted to visualize this multi-dimensional problem.

His introduction of the box that carries his name today, was a very useful way to represent economic efficiencies and distributions, allowing for the visualization and analysis of how different allocations of resources can lead to Pareto optimal outcomes, becoming a fundamental tool in microeconomics.

'Space we can recover, lost time never'– NAPOLEON[10]

Let's address then the optimization of learning through time first: The applicability of Edgeworth's box to our learning framework *lies first in its ability to illustrate the optimal allocation of learning resources over time,* ensuring that learning is efficient and effective within a given system. Inspired by Edgeworth's framework, the diagram is built with two opposing corners.

On the first one (learning supply side):

- *The origin in the lower-left corner* marks the beginning of the parasystemic learning system

- *It faces the parasystemic demand for learning,* which represents the need for problem-solving processes.

- *The vertical axis measures the generative capability* of the parasystem, while the *horizontal axis gauges its cognitive inferential capacity*

On the opposite corner *(challenge demand side):*

- *At the upper right corner, we find the characterization of the problems* to be tackled by the system—this is our learning demand or, the supply of problems.

- *The vertical axis here correlates with the frequency* or repeatability of the problems produced by the system.

- *The horizontal axis, on the other hand, measures their variability,* spawned from the diversity and uncertainty inherent in the system's variables.

To construct an Edgeworth box for this scenario, we introduce a couple of critical assumptions:

---

a) *An increase in problem repeatability reduces the need for*
   generative capacity
b) *Greater problem variability diminishes the usefulness of a knowledge-based inference system*

These assumptions hold a high correlation with empirical evidence across various fields:

1) The notion that problem repeatability reduces the need for generative capacity is reasonable. Across disciplines, *repeated problems lead to the development of standard responses:*

- *Mass production of identical parts results in the creation of injection molds,* seeking both efficiency and quality
- *Biological systems have set 'reflexes' to face common dangers*

2) *Greater problem variability diminishes the usefulness of a knowledge-based inference system,* rule-based systems thrive on predictability

Defined in this manner, *the strategic learning tracking map* delineates *the efficiency of the parasystem in resolving evolving problems through time.* The area is spanned by snapshots of two convex curves *(intersecting or not)* at different points in time:

- *The curves stretching from left to right represent a parasystemic learning function evolving through time.* As we move further from the origin, the isoquants signify an increased learning capacity *(at a cost). Their convexity conveys a balanced mix of learning, more potent than an approach focused on one type.*

COLLECTIVE LEARNING STRATEGIC TRACKING MAP

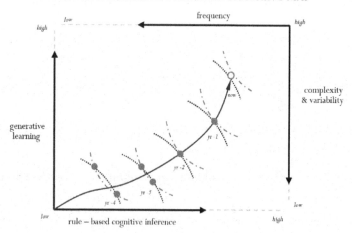

- *The isoquants running from right to left represent shifting problem functions.* The nearer to their origin they are, *they demand faster, more complex solutions.* Our choice of the convexity of problems becomes interesting. A balanced mix of issues *(in terms of variability and frequency) tends to be less challenging to solve than highly skewed issues, benefiting from specialization*

The most fascinating part of employing an Edgeworth box as described is identifying the optimal path under Pareto's criterion after qualitatively modeling the curves for the system under analysis.

This path, consisting of all the tangency points between the two isoquant families, charts the trajectory of optimal learning utilization. At any point on this curve, *it would be impossible to outpace the quality and speed of the parasystemic learning capacity, given the specific problem set at that time.*

PARETO – EFFICIENT LEARNING PATH OVER TIME

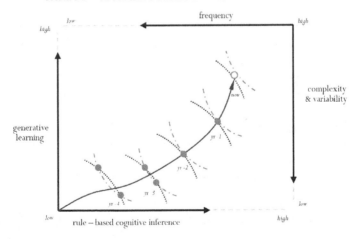

95

Tracing the curve from right to left transitions from a position of minimal benefits *(slow response times or poor solution quality)*, at potentially limited costs to a scenario of significant benefits that necessitates substantial investment in learning.

The Pareto Path should ideally be a simple line. The presence of an area at any given time indicates a *'learning buffer'* - a variety of learning combinations available at a lower utility cost. *This is not necessarily negative,* especially if the marginal cost of resources needed to generate this excess learning capacity is:

- *Not wasted on ineffective research, processes, or systems.*
- *Utilized to exceed consumer expectations, challenging competitors with superior processes and products*
- *Used as a reserve to handle abrupt shifts in the problem curve*

The last point is particularly important. *There must be a buffer.*

AVOIDING A COLLECTIVE LEARNING FAILURE EVENT

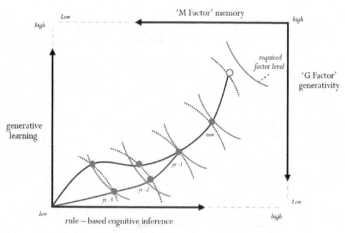

The best strategy is to position the organization along this trajectory, while building and deploying discretional buffers to generate competitive momentum.

When executed effectively, this approach not only sustains the *'defensive buffer'* but also transforms it into a *'competitive moat',* ultimately evolving into a fundamental strategic asset.

'In any series of elements to be controlled, a small fraction of elements, always accounts for a large fraction in terms of effect' – *VILFREDO PARETO*[8]

When addressing the critical question of estimating the resources needed to align an organization with the optimal collective learning path, we fully recognize that this is a multivariate problem. As Pareto himself would remind us, a few key elements typically have the majority of the impact.

Acknowledging that this multivariate, multidimensional optimization problem exists within a hypercube, let's simplify it into two primary types of investment buckets, each highly correlated with a specific type of learning.

This approach allows us to propose a different bidimensional projection of the learning optimization problem:

- *The lower left corner represents the production of learning over time,* achieving the milestones for optimal learning.

- *The upper corner corresponds to the cost of two simplified factors of production:*

  - *The horizontal axis corresponds to what we term 'M type' Memoristic Factors,* enhancing organizational memory and formalized processes. *These might include technical training, standardization investments, and rule-based systems*

- *The vertical axis represents 'G type' factors* that primarily promote option generation and exploratory testing. *These encourage collective creativity, encompassing a broadening of job design, flexible experimentation, and enhanced communication*

The interplay between these newly defined 'G' and 'M' investment factor axes warrants discussion. Specifically, the natural limitations of resources imply that allocating resources to one type of learning diminishes their availability for the other.

Convexity is also a relevant consideration, indicating that a balanced mix of these factors is more efficient than relying exclusively on one. Cognitive inference becomes more challenging without the ability to generate options. *Similarly, generative capabilities are most effective upon a robust foundation of stored knowledge.*

PLANNING GENERATIVE AND MEMORISTIC LEVELS

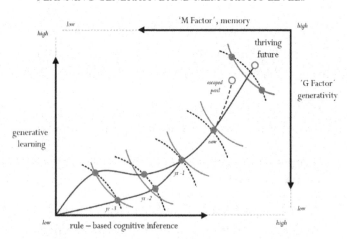

The isoquants representing investment would differ for each organization. The impact of investments in trial-based learning *(generativity)* and *cognitive inference* is shaped by several factors.

These include the organization's culture, the sophistication of its information systems, and the dynamics of power within the organization, among other elements.

'A most powerful knight, Sir Money is...'– QUEVEDO[11]

Turning to the aspects of finance and utility, let's consider a conservative organization. Such an entity might easily adopt formalization mechanisms while resisting generative design factors. Each strategy incurs its own implicit costs, as depicted by the isoquants, *reflecting the varying expenses associated with favoring one learning paradigm over another.*

PLANNING 'G' AND 'M' FACTORS THROUGH TIME

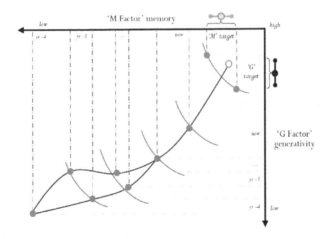

The isoquants, unique to each organization, would illustrate the varying influences on functions like trial-based learning (generativity) and cognitive inference.

These functions are shaped by factors such as culture, the state of information systems, and internal power dynamics. For instance, a risk-averse entity might readily adopt formalization mechanisms but resist generative design factors.

Each approach entails implicit costs, which the isoquants represent: *The differing expenses involved in favoring one learning paradigm over another.*

Consequently, an optimal balance trajectory can be established:

> *This trajectory delineates, for a given level of a learning paradigm, the maximum feasible extent of the complementary paradigm.*

SETTING INVESTMENT FACTOR TARGETS

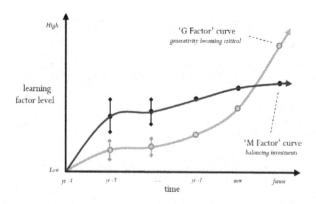

This 'optimums' curve, from the perspective of Pareto, identifies points where, considering the organization's character and current structure, the marginal substitution rates between different learning paradigms are equalized.

The tracking map highlights trade-offs in promoting learning factors, such as the interdependence between the effectiveness of an investment and the entity's readiness for it.

However, it does not specify the levels of each factor to be pursued.

To optimize learning efficiency while minimizing associated costs, *we need a concept similar to the 'great utility-possibility curve'* *found in economics.* This curve represents the combinations of goods and services that can be produced in an economy, given its technological capabilities and resource availability.

In the context of organizational learning, we propose the 'Learning-Designability' frontier.

THE LEARNING – DESIGNABILITY FRONTIER

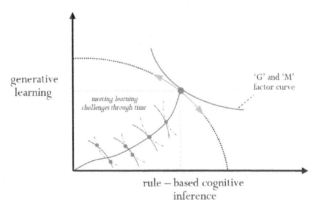

This facilitates the visualization of a double optimization problem, where the goal is to determine the efficient mix of paradigms, *improving both learning costs and benefits.*

The curves are constructed in the following way: For each level of promotion of the generative paradigm, the maximum levels of production of the cognitive paradigm are obtained from the available resources and restrictions.

This frontier delineates a realistic spectrum of learning promotion possibilities and its boundaries:

- Within the limitations of this frontier, the tangency point with the family of learning utility curves must be found—*curves that represent higher levels of solution quality or shorter times as they move away from the origin*

- The slope of the tangent line to the highest-value indifference curve represents the 'marginal rate of transformation' in learning paradigms

The optimal learning mix for a parasystem is identified at this point of tangency, dictating the proportions that will sit concurrently on the trajectory of optimal learning utilization and the path of optimal balance of design factors

---

In Economics, the curve shows the relationship between the maximization of utility and the minimization of relative production factor costs.

Similarly, in the learning case there is <u>no guaranteed relationship between costs and benefits,</u> so these are also two separate optimization problems.

What is sought is the uniqueness in the solution, the one that simultaneously satisfies the two sets of optimal solutions from each perspective.

Restating this key observation: When designing learning organizations, there is no direct dependency between costs and benefits. The collective system need to be able to absorb that investment, *be it people, processes, or information technology.*

This is the intuition that the *'Learning - Designability'* Frontier should provide to the designer of learning organizations. Readiness matters, and to achieve some levels of higher learning, the frontier needs to be expanded.

The collective learning marginal utility function is essential:

- *What is the cost of having a low 'L&D' ceiling,* i.e., a low room to maneuver and affect learning?
- *How do we expand the 'L&D' frontier,* if the competitive environment created a learning gap?
- *Under what crisis scenarios we need to commit learning resources (at risk)* compromising short-term ROI?

Elaborating on that last point, the model will be useful *to visualize 'clinical pictures' of learning over time,* allowing the diagnosis of some basic learning diseases, suggesting the actions to implement the corresponding corrections.

Multivariate Optimization

Recapping on the visualization methodology proposed to diagnose the problem, we are leaning heavily in time-tested microeconomic frameworks that provide both a theoretical foundation to seek the optimal solution *(not the scope of this work),* but the visualization tools and principles behind the key aspects of solving for the optimization problem.

It is in the framing of these projections of the learning 'hypercube' where the value for the learning designer lies: *isolating the key factors and understanding their interaction dynamics.*

So, in summary, parasystemic learning can be visualized as a function of:

- *Learning supply and demand curves across every realm*

- Tracking *the attainment of optimal learning through time*

- Understanding the *relationship between learning investments ('G vs. M' factors) and expected results*

- Mapping out the required investments through time *(and how to improve their effectiveness)*

- Setting *'Learning - Designability'* frontiers, where investments beyond readiness may yield no results

The proposed diagnostic model not only aids in assessing and mapping the interaction among parasystemic variables *but also exposes the need for an organizational learning metasystem.*

***

In the following section, the concept and purpose of the organizational learning metasystem will be explored. *As a living biological entity operates, without the need of a explaining theory,* organizations large or small, smart or stagnant, adapt somehow and evolve. *An overarching learning metasystem is at work.*

6

METASYSTEM: THE ORCHESTRATOR

Who is driving the 'G' and 'M' factors...

UNTIL NOW, WE HAVE ONLY EXAMINED FEATURES of learning subsystems within organizations. These entities embody the primary capacity for reactive or adaptive learning associated with each organizational process. We've explored how a blend of learning paradigms—generation and testing, or rule-based—is crucial for addressing either innovative or repetitive challenges.

Additionally, we discussed that these paradigms are not independent. Rather, they are constrained by interdependent design factors. For example, *changing the proportion of one learning paradigm inevitably influences the resources available for the other mode ('G' vs. 'M' mix).*

However, a critical nuance was left unaddressed. The balance point of a learning subsystem does not necessarily equate to an optimal state. Often, it may diverge from the ideal, since the primary goal of these subsystems is to adapt a process to specific parameters through adaptive learning.

The question then arises: who or what guides this convergence between organizational needs and realities? Under our framework, this vital role is played by the Organizational Learning Metasystem. This overarching entity functions as a second-tier system, where mostly generative learning takes place. *It optimizes and reshapes the parasystems.*

THE NEED FOR A COMPENSATORY METASYSTEM

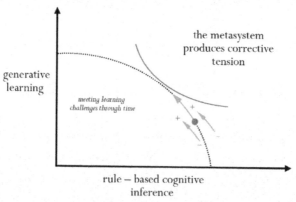

Just as organizational processes are interrelated, so too are learning subsystems. These interconnections occur at two levels: sensory *(or perceptual)* and parametric *(or prescriptive)*.

To comprehend the sensory level, let's recall that while we have been considering organizational processes in isolation to analyze their associated learning structures. The underlying processes are deeply interconnected in practice. They are not just linked through input and output flows but also through other processes *(planning, contingency management, among others).*

This interconnectivity implies that parasystems are aware of variables beyond their own processes, in particular from neighboring subsystems. We refer to these connections as *pre-generative learning points.* And they are a key input to the metasystem.

ORGANIZATIONAL LEARNING METASYSTEM

To manage these interfaces adeptly, there must be a supervisory function that examines how one system's goals affect another and vice versa.

The metasystem in an organization acts like a central command center. It oversees various learning processes, ensuring they align with the organization's goals. Think of it as a senior officer who oversees different teams, making sure everyone works effectively towards a common objective.

For instance, in a government, the metasystem might analyze trade data, public opinion polls and external 'benchmark' metrics, contrasting them with the results obtained by each branch of the government to guide the executives team on learning rate and strategy adjustments.

To exemplify, let's think about two neighboring countries —with deep economic ties, but independent from each other.

- *Who makes complex decision such as enabling a trade-free zone?*

- *How to control migration flows, irrespective of how one country experiments it vis-à-vis the other?*

Surely, these initiatives are not decided and implemented just on their own at the borders between the entities:

- A complex decision of this nature, even though its implementation could be straightforward, implies:
- modifying paradigms of the countries involved *(realms),* the operations of the customs systems, and potentially creating new contact points *(connections)*

- The perspective needed to consider all inputs is not present at the border units – despite being the most exposed, driving feedback on a daily basis

- It is typically a 'higher-level' decision where each government had to examine the influence that such a measure would have on all sectors of its population,

  .. Modify the operating parameters (criteria) of several interrelated processes and stakeholders, and

  .. Monitor the process to ensure objectives are being accomplished, or intervene and/or improve the system

The metasystem operates in a similar manner. It aggregates information from each learning subsystem, particularly the pre-generative points sitting at the boundary between realms and performs two functions: *integration and redistribution.*

On the integration side, its main task is to aggregate environmental information, performance data, and the organization's objectives *(inputs to the system),* producing sets of scenarios to assess the performance of the parasystems.

When it comes to the redistribution angle, the metasystem needs to revise the resources and suggested structural, parametric modifications the parasystems will use to learn and adjust operational processes in the next learning cycle.

In the ideal state, these two actions by the metasystem should cause dynamic transformations in the responses and the structure of the organizational parasystems.

Think about a bank that is late adapting rates and collections as part of a business cycle.

- As interests go up, risk takers will flock to the institution that is slowest to adapt their pricing and underwriting policies.
- If collections are late to kick in as well, you have potentially a perfect storm caused by three parasystems associated to pricing, underwriting and collections.
- The metasystem then determines what improvements the parasystems need, depending upon the gap.

For that, the metasystem first aggregates external data, parasystem's outputs, and pre-generative learning points *(typically revealing early gaps, like a sudden rise in underwriting activity or spikes in early collections).*

In sequence, it integrates the scenarios to optimize the system, given resource constraints *(people, systems, processes).*

HOW THE METASYSTEM ACTS

The term *metasystem* is particularly apt if one considers that it is a system *beyond* the 'base' learning parasystem, performing a similar role on them as they perform on their associated units. *Its focus is addressing the needs of parasystems (not operational units):*

- *What are the functions of the learning metasystem?*
- *Why does it learn differently than parasystems?*

To answer these questions, let's consider the situation *depicted below:* a parasystem's output does not align anymore with new problems. *The metasystem acts to correct this situation.*

FAKE EQUILIBRIUMS: THE LEARNING 'DUTCH DISEASE' 1

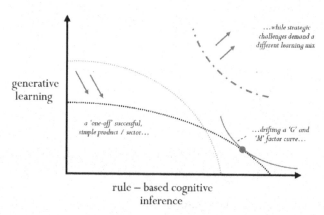

The metasystem's objective is 'simply' to align the marginal rate of substitution *between 'learning consumption' and 'learning production'* with the marginal rate of production of 'G' *(option generation)* and 'M' *(memory and process formalization)* factors.

Achieving an optimal intersection of these variables, as visualized prior in an Edgeworth Box, ensures the parasystem reaches its Pareto efficient point, where no further improvements can be made without causing a trade-off.

But... could one seriously argue that an organizational system will act in response to an optimization criterion like Pareto's?

And Economic Theory provides sound advice: *the system does not act by applying the criterion. It only behaves as if it were doing so.*

This assumption, in the case of the learning metasystem, is based on a key notion in cybernetic systems theory, where there is a seldom-mentioned concept within the organizational realm: *Energy.*

Energy: The premise we propose is that learning models get transformed through energy dynamics, instead of the traditional notion of 'cost-benefit' analyses.
There are several advantages to thinking in terms of energy:

- In physical systems, the build-up of potential energy *creates a tension or potential differential*
- *This potential energy will convert into kinetic energy, facilitating change,* once the tension overcomes the system's inertia
- The process will halt at the new potential level *due to resistance (frictional) forces or through an inelastic collision,* causing structural deformation

The energy concept also compels designers to think in terms of material transformation, *achieving both reusable and non-reusable outcomes, such as structural changes and 'heat'*

'The sum of kinetic energy and potential energy in the whole of nature is constant'- VON HELMHOLTZ²

Cybernetic systems theory, in simple terms, is about how systems self-regulate and maintain energy stability. In our organization, this means how different parasystems adjust to stay on track towards our goals.

Generally speaking, all systems *have a characteristic energy function around which the system's stability criteria are defined:*

- Systems stabilize around either *local or absolute minima of their energy function*
- Transitory instabilities *are caused by situations that create accumulations of potential energy*
- These overcome the system's inherent inertia and *trigger a process of change characterized by the conversion of this potential energy into kinetic energy.*
- This change process typically *results in the system reaching a new equilibrium state that has less energy than before*

Various events can manifest parallels of this theory in the organizational realm. *For instance, a system (organization) might undergo an inelastic collision, which would alter its structural framework (structure). Most of the generated kinetic energy is used in the deformation process, with a small portion dissipating as heat.*

Now, how can we link the energy framework to explain the way in which the metasystem changes 'set' parasystems? Imagine the learning oversight in an organization as a battery. Just like a battery stores and releases energy, the organization accumulates tension *(stores energy)* as there are gaps, and then applies it *(releases energy)*, overcoming set parasystem patterns, to improve learning and evolve.

Let's visualize again our unbalanced parasystem. The situation may correspond to a unit experiencing significant environmental change, altering the nature of problems the parasystem must address.

HOW THE METASYSTEM OPERATES

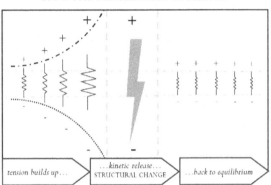

tension builds up... | ...kinetic release... STRUCTURAL CHANGE | ...back to equilibrium

The essence is that this change starts generating significant tension in the system, *due to a growing disparity between the learning capacity of the parasystem and the requirements of the process.*

> **Tension:** It could be said that the tension thus defined coincides with Senge's concept of 'creative tension,' which is represented as an elongated elastic band stretched by the difference between aspirations and realities.

The metasystem detects this anomaly, which could eventually threaten the stability of the associated process and cause a potential crisis in the related chain of processes.

In response, the metasystem adjusts parameters to feed back into the troubled parasystem. It thus acts as a redistributor of the tension, concentrating it on those parasystems where the imbalance creates energy accumulation.

However, the change is not immediate. The parasystems *(and underlying systems)* have an already established structure, which generates an intrinsic inertia that blocks any attempt at change.

The metasystem continues to increase parametric tension to compensate, until accumulated potential energy reaches a level that overcomes this inertia, inducing a change process.

Resistance: Just as in the prior example, the notion of inertia in learning organizations can be effectively articulated also through the lens of barriers to learning - concepts thoroughly examined by Chris Argyris in his work, *'Overcoming Organizational Defenses.'* This alternative perspective also offers actionable insights for organizations striving for a learning culture.

The pattern graphically establishes an analogy with high-voltage electrical conduction and the use of insulators.

In overload situations, the potential increases progressively until it is sufficient to overcome the air's dielectric resistance, turning it into a conductive medium. *A large spark jumps from one cable to another, usually destroying the tension insulator (resistance).*

The accumulated potential energy, represented as a voltage differential, transforms into plasma (*kinetic energy*). After the event, the structure has changed: *the potential energy is minimal, inertia is low, and the transformed system is stable once again.*

When we talk about *'potential energy'* in the learning context, *we mean the increased incentive to realign untapped knowledge and skills within the organization.* *'Kinetic energy'* refers to the *active use of this knowledge to make changes and progress*

Likewise, in the case of learning parasystems, the accumulation of parametric tension, channeled by the metasystem, *eventually breaks down the structures resisting change:*

- The process may be more or less intense, but if effective, the released kinetic energy creates the necessary structural modifications

- The larger the resistance, the lower the efficiency of the process, incremental changes may happen swiftly, while larger ones be associated with more friction:

  - Some are *'surgical,'* achieving efficient alignment of parasystemic learning features with assessed needs

  - In other instances, changes will face more resistance, there will be a significant amount of kinetic energy dissipated, which translates to wasted resources

- And, occasionally, the system may not arrive at a satisfactory end-state, requiring further adjustments

'If you want to find the secrets of the universe, think in terms of energy, frequency, and vibration'- TESLA[3]

The crucial takeaway is that the model suggests adding generative learning, unlike incremental inference learning, is not of an incremental nature but rather impulsive.

A successful, strong impact on the perceptual system consequently alters how the entity interprets reality from that point forward. *An organizational epiphany.*

Structures Enabling Metasystemic Learning

The basis for understanding the difference between parasystemic learning *(typically reactive, supervised)* and metasystemic learning *(mostly generative, unsupervised)* lies here:

- The metasystem has the ability to monitor both:
    - First-level variables *(e.g. environmental conditions)*
    - Granular outcomes of the parasystems across the collective, *and the variance vis a vis training targets*
- It also consumes information about the network weights *(connection strength)*
- It processes the constraints in the system, as neither network resources nor training costs are unlimited
- Its output consists of parameter sets that will govern the structure and functioning of adaptive parasystems

- There are no external parameters that regulate metasystems' training. *It self-regulates.*

How can a learning system operate without a reference point? The metasystem's structure *is not dependent on external parameters but can generate and revise its own,* seeking stability.

This unique attribute makes it distinctive with most parasystemic learning paradigms. Through an AI framework, called *constraint propagation,* problems are solved by *focusing attention on the constraints of the problem.*

Through selective attention procedures on these constraints, something essential is achieved in the metasystem:

Global Systemic Consistency

This understanding of metasystemic learning aligns with the integrative, configuration function identified earlier.

By focusing on result quality and structural and learning cost constraints and consolidating them, it's possible to generate an internal matrix of parameters to self-regulate the system's functioning.

- *Additional parasystemic learning layers*
- *Feature specialization,* competing approaches
- *Collection & annotation of additional training data*

In AI, this process is called the *Goal Reduction Paradigm,* where network stability and optimal clustering are achieved through constraint propagation. These clusters will enable the analysis of options to generate parameter sets to enhance the learning of each parasystem.

It is worth noting that the organizational learning system, even at this high level, is inherently distributed.

Its central representation means only to represent its connectivity to all the parts. It is not an algorithmic expression holding the optimization of all the collective learning system.

From this representation or pattern, specific goals are generated that will correspond to the individual patterns governing each parasystem.

The impulsive nature of this process, *accumulating differences, creating tension, and instigating change,* must not be overlooked.

This consideration is crucial for designers of learning organizations. The metasystem would be less disruptive if the frequency of corrective impulses is higher. This will result in shorter imbalances threatening internal equilibrium.

In design terms, there is a need to create structures capable of efficiently accumulating tension—a sort of organizational 'potential energy stores', a capacitor or battery of sorts, that can gather energy incrementally and release the amplified tension caused by a parasystem's maladaptation over time, overcoming inertia and thus enabling effective transformation and reducing the trigger time for change processes.

Lowering Resistance: Fostering Learning Adaptability

In addition to the ability to accumulate energy, it is important to aim for the design of low-inertia parasystems that demonstrate higher receptivity and flexibility to parametric changes.

The transparency provided by the parasystems must be very high.

The quality of learning metrics and their correct impact attribution will dictate the accuracy of the metasystem's second-level corrective processes.

How many organizations have failed due to significant deficiencies in their metasystemic learning? It's hard to say.

However, many failing companies appear to avoid creating tensions in response to environmental changes. Consequently, they never manage to spark revitalizing impulses or did so too late. *Many cases in the literature, such as the American automotive industry documented in chapter 2, appear rooted in weak learning metasystems.*

In cases of metasystem failure, when the rate of corrective impulses to adapt the parasystems falls below the rate of environmental changes, organizations lose competitiveness. *Conversely, if it's above that threshold, they gain competitiveness.*

Moreover, an organization's generative learning often changes the surrounding environment, acting as a catalyst that accelerates the rate of environmental changes.

Consequently, the development of disruptive learning systems by a key player within a sector *creates rapidly a hostile,*

'Darwinian' environment, with rising stakes and highly charged, enticing change for all participants and new entrants:

- Tensions will increase rapidly across all participants,

- Some organizations will trigger lightning-bolt changes, while adapting to new situations

- Others, late to recognize their slow metasystems or high inertia parasystems lack effective responses (fading away or imploding)

How can organizations best prepare for those transformation storms? The objective being to emerge reinvented - nimbler, smarter, more adaptable. The alternative is to give in to less competitive strongholds or succumb unable to change.

***

Next, we will take a look at the key structural qualities of organizational learning and its layered nature, akin to the sails and engines required to successfully maneuver in rough learning waters.

7
———

UNDERLYING STRUCTURES
Layers of Learning Networks

T HE FOUNDATIONAL STRUCTURES that support collective learning play a pivotal role in an organization's trajectory towards success or failure.

Key adaptation networks, strategically integrated with essential units and core competencies, are instrumental in shaping the organization's future. Mirroring nature's intricacies, we compare these networks' data processing to the coordinated rhythms of the communication channels of a beehive or the guiding pheromones of an ant colony, which both ensure survival and competitiveness.

Within organizations, data connections and knowledge repositories are not static; they are evolving continuously , adapting to both internal dynamics and external changes. Our exploration focuses on these networks, their interplay and adaptability in an ever-changing business landscape.

COLLECTIVE LEARNING:
IT IS ALL ABOUT THE NETWORK

We have previously identified two key reasons for the scarcity of Organizational Learning models:

1. *The dominance of the rational learning paradigm,* which, while helpful in addressing individual learning to some degree, has limited applicability to collective learning.

2. *The complexity of addressing collective learning,* related fields such as psychology, focus on individual learning, overshadowing the study of group learning dynamics.

Such a focus has led to the study of collective learning through the lens of individual members, *rather than understanding it as an integrated, connected whole.*

In a learning network, the knowledge lies in the connections, not in the individual processing nodes. Organizational learning is distinct from the mere sum of its parts. We describe it not necessarily as 'greater' — *a term often used to imply synergies* — but as fundamentally 'different'.

Could an imaginary extraterrestrial entomologist, analyzing only a single earth bee, deduce that they are capable of living in complex colonies, performing location decisions, task allocation — *from food foraging to storage, distribution, and defense?*

Such an analysis of an isolated worker bee would not reveal the most important capabilities of their species' successful evolutionary path.

To understand their biological competitiveness, *it's necessary to analyze the structure of the hive, as a living system of its own, abstracting from its individual member capabilities.*

To understand a collective, we need to step back and look at its morphology and behaviors, gathering perspective on:

- How key decisions are made in the collective?
    - *Establishment*
    - *competition*
- What structures are critical?
    - *resource gathering*
    - *allocation*
- What roles do members perform?
    - *general roles*
    - *specialization*
- How do members communicate?
    - *information transmission*
    - *generational learning*

From ants and bees to complex multinational corporations, it is important to understand the 'whole' and then the parts.

The tendency to focus on the trees, while missing the forest, may be the main cause of the void of structural models in Organizational Learning.

Therefore, this section will emphasize the use of a broad perspective—a 'wide-angle lens'— shifting the focus from individual learning to the structures themselves as a whole, seeking for parasystems and metasystems that appear to shape the behavior of the collective.

PARASYSTEMIC LEARNING

Consider an organization. *A natural way to visualize it is as a grid of interrelated individuals interacting with each other.*

The term 'grid' is particularly apt, as it suggests the existence of a network of connections linking these individuals. The nature of the relations between them is diverse, depending on their position within the grid, which is essentially a mesh of:

- Power relations
- Procedures
- Communications
- Decision-making
- Information-technology

Building on this reticular vision, topological considerations arise: Are all nodes connected, operating effectively? Not all of them may be interconnected as needed…

In fact, it's possible that when it comes to learning very few are.

INTERCONNECTING LEARNING LAYERS

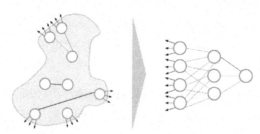

FROM: individuals and their teams, randomly striving to think together…

…TO: designing organizations based on critical feature analysis

On the left, we have the *'as-is'* view. *With a few exceptions (e.g., structured R&D), learning exchanges may appear random and elusive,* morphing dynamically, depending on individual characteristics and their roles at any given moment in time.

Sometimes, data appears to flow through power structures. In other cases, collaborative informal communication prevail. *What is going on?*

Once we adopt this view of the organization, our focus shifts from individuals to the connections between them.

It's like seeing the network as lines meeting at points, rather than points connected by lines. When the nodes cease to be the center of attention, the structure formed by the connections becomes apparent – *and we can optimize it.*

'At times is seems these canals extend as thin black lines and seen with such certainty that one cannot doubt their reality'- SCHIAPARELLI[1]

To better visualize these learning connections, let's think of them as information channels, *or 'canali' as Schiaparelli would call the canals he thought connected Mars' imaginary cities.* And, much like his visions of potential Martian life fueled an incredible interest in Mars, woven information channels, that 'learn' promise great attention. Fortunately, the theoretical basis of collective learning is mathematically sound.

If more data flows through one channel than another, pertaining a particular aspect of a given problem, it will be represented by a proportionally thicker line.

The process activities both generate and need information for control. This need is shown by the growing number of connections between the system and the parasystemic network. Depending on each task's complexity, there may be one or several pathways linking the process to this network.

The topology of the network, along with the density of specific information channels, should align with the characteristics of the problems being solved.

It's clear that the system being represented serves the same functions as the learning subsystems analyzed in the previous section. *They are units of distributed information processing.*

When viewed as a static image, like a photograph, the structure shows the learning achieved by the subsystem so far, particularly in how the process creates and uses information.

To grasp how the network produces suitable responses, let's reconsider the concept of nodes. Here, nodes are not just points on the organizational grid representing individuals, but specialized processing units focusing on specific features. *Here, a node could represent the analysis of a team or even part of a researcher's work.*

So what do these nodes represent? *Nodes serve as primary information concentration points, performing three key functions:*

1. *Aggregating information* from incoming paths
2. *Identifying specific patterns* in that information
3. *Propagating the processed information (i.e., the identified pattern)* to other nodes

The primary roles of the nodes, capturing and sharing information, are straightforward, given that the network's most evident function is to act as an information capture and propagation structure.

The second function involves the network's ability to interpret data.

Given a specific set of input variables related to a task and based on the weights of the connections between them, set during training, nodes on a layer may identify certain patterns. *In this model, interpreted information means recognizing specific node 'firing' patterns.*

PATTERNS: DO NOT MISS THE LINKS FOR THE NODES

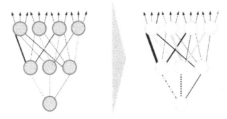

GROUP AND LAYER teams, according   ...AND ANALYZE CONNECTIVITY
to learning role and feature focus ...   among teams and their models

Thus, whether a pattern exactly matches a known response or not, the parasystemic function activates, *either aligning input with the situation or creating a new option.*

Certainly, in complex systems, pattern recognition plays a critical role, but it's not always straightforward. An input pattern might either be something previously encountered or a novel one demanding varying levels of action.

Pattern identification typically involves a second layer that process the features identified by the first one.

And this feature recognition structure can be replicated successively, as upper layers specialize in extracting *(or filtering)* more insights. The multi-layered structure of the parasystems is inherently robust, due to its distributed design.

> *Parasystemic learning is not a standalone function in any particular node; it's an emergent property of this entire information processing parasystem.*

This multi-layer nature allows for the construction of increasingly complex patterns, *not only specializing vertically,* but connecting to neighboring units, contributing to a holistic understanding of interrelated processes.

'Every problem must be considered from every angle, whether practical or impractical, to arrive at a proper solution'- HOLLERITH[2]

Parasystemic learning enable various perspectives in organizations.

In the ideal situation, every operational unit would be supported by arrays of learning individuals or teams, focused on recognized critical features *(and with the ability to explore new ones),* backed up by proper processes and systems.

These units offer recommendations, advance while receiving feedback, and are rewarded for accurate predictions.

This enables a higher level of collective intelligence *(not only different than individual learning but superior)*, based on:

- improved featurization of the input vector *(field data)*

- the freedom of teams to look at selective features (from all the input to aggregate their recommendations

- fact-based feedback and healthy competition to come with the best categorization patterns

At third-level patterns and beyond, we deal with complex scenarios that impact different parts of the system.

Post-implementation, there is an evaluative phase where actions are assessed against desired outcomes, allowing for either the reinforcing or weakening the informational pathways that led to those actions, depending on their success.

Structures of Parasystemic Learning

It's worth noting that in this array, we are not restricted to rule-based learning – it is actually compatible with it and can help increase the generation of new options.

What if the pattern isn't recognizable at any given layer? A properly functioning array would showcase its adaptability by transitioning from a rule-based inference mechanism to one of generation and testing.

Unrecognizable patterns still evoke responses; they stimulate alternative pathways based on partial similarities to known tasks or procedures.

This multi-layered architecture enables the gradual recognition of more complex features. It specializes vertically and also connects to neighboring units, aiding in a comprehensive understanding of interconnected processes.

PARASYSTEM'S LAYERS SUPPORTING CORE PROCESSES

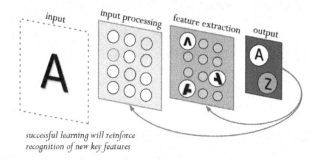

successful learning will reinforce recognition of new key features

Certainly, in the case of complex pattern recognition, the parasystem may consider various trajectories *(hypothesis)*. There are multiple pathways that could respond to an incoming pattern. And there may be emerging features that are better at discerning new patterns. This is the strength of a collective learning array.

Each of these alternatives recognizes partial similarities with first and second-level tasks and procedures.

These options are then rigorously evaluated against system-desired parameters, and the most closely aligned one is selected for implementation.

The chosen alternative is evaluated then, to either strengthen its use in the future or reduce it if it doesn't meet expectations.

The structural paradigm of parasystemic learning we've outlined possesses four key features:

1. It is adaptive, accommodating both rule-based and generative paradigms.
2. Its learning is supervised, with the network being trained on new cases and adapting its channels accordingly.
3. The structure is directly influenced by the quality of the learning process, which can either strengthen or weaken its informational pathways.
4. In cases where the existing structure is inadequate for problem-solving, the metasystem intervenes.

This intervention can lead to significant network adjustments, ranging from pathway realignments to the creation of new analytical layers, or shifts in rule persistence and network generativity.

Building on these features, we must consider the critical factors to evaluating learning within this model:

- *The pattern-recognition capability of individual layers.*

- *The degree of connectivity between these layers.*

- *The overall number of processing elements and their interconnections.*

Enhancing either of one of these factors can significantly amplify the network's generative capacity and memory, leading to reduced response times. The system's information bandwidth must be managed to ensure it does not exceed the network's capacity to process and utilize it effectively.

PARASYSTEM'S LAYERS SUPPORTING CORE PROCESSES

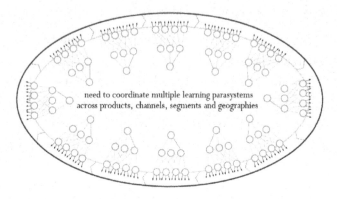

So, how would one visualize the parasystems within an organization? Picture a cycle where specialized parasystems handle specific organizational core processes:

Within this cycle, specialized parasystems cater to specific processes in the business chain, catering to their respective units and neighboring processes.

These parasystems are visualized as information capture and processing networks, where lower levels recognize task-associated patterns, and higher levels deal with variables descriptive of the entire process.

Metasystemic Learning

Moving beyond parasystemic learning, one naturally arrives at metasystemic learning.

The learning methods at this higher level differ significantly. This difference lays the groundwork for nuanced paradigms that can guide the entire collective adaptation capability.

In the case of a parasystemic network, each processing node operates under a pre-defined goal, which is shaped by externally generated parameters:

- Imagine a 'teacher' setting right and wrong, satisfied only when desired changes are achieved.
- Repeatedly reviewing past experiences, the system develops heuristics to tackle future problems.
- The system is memory-intensive. Although not quite rule-based, it relies extensively on past experiences.

In contrast, the metasystem must independently establish its guidelines, creating them based on new situation evaluations and setting goals for its specialized parasystems.

These alternatives undergo evaluation, and the metasystem implements the most effective one, based on the effectiveness of its current parameters.

This flexibility and layered assessment show the system's strength and its ability to handle complex situations.

When focusing on action evaluation, *organizing the metasystem's parameters in a goal-tree structure becomes crucial:*

- *performance:* monitoring the parasystems results against predefined goals, using their output as a benchmark.
- *data-driven adjustments:* triggering training refinements and to fine-tune learning outcomes
- *targeted interventions:* the metasystem may point to evaluate specific changes or alternatives

Structures of Metasystemic Learning

Consider the strategic planning process within a corporation as an illustrative example.

- At first glance, metasystem roles seem aligned with the activities unfolding during planning.
- The process appears to be neatly composed by a sequence of tasks following each other over time.

In practice, strategic planning often turns into a 'political model.' It becomes a battlefield where organizational units compete to assert their views, aiming to secure more resources or negotiate less stringent objectives.

In the neural model, the metasystem effectively navigates the complexities of strategic planning for learning. By integrating diverse inputs and balancing competing interests. It functions as an advanced decision-making hub, guiding the organization towards cohesive, strategic actions.

THE METASYSTEM'S INTEGRATING FUNCTION

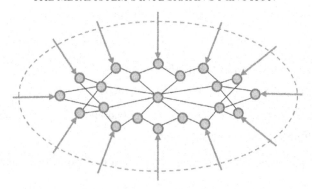

clustering parasystems learning issues and patterns for decision-makers

What is fascinating, is how this scenario naturally gravitates back to the concept of a network—specifically, kind of a *'star network'* topology that links everyone to everyone, enabling the flow of communication concerning objectives and needs, and allowing competition among them to manifest.

In the context of a metasystemic network, one of the primary objectives is to generate a prescriptive description of the organization.

The metasystem's aim is to clearly demonstrate how learning affects the organization by comparing goals, limitations, and performance, thereby illustrating the causal factors affecting learning in various areas.

The metasystem sets specific guidelines for each parasystem based on these parameters. Think of it, initially, as a *'parasystem for parasystems.'*

It manages the learning processes by assessing how well the parasystem can handle current problems, considering both response time and solution quality.

However, its learning methodology and execution approach is different, as we brought up in the previous chapter:

- *its learning is unsupervised; based on clustering input data,* there's no external *'teacher,'* often without specific guidance on what to predict, *just seeking similar types of patterns and linking it to results.*

- *Its actions can be quite impulsive and sudden, especially when it needs to address major issues by pushing parasystems towards more efficient problem-solving methods.*

Effective outcomes rely on the metasystem's ability to exert pressure, the adaptability of parasystems to change, and feedback velocity, which enables reinforcing successful actions and corrects unsuccessful ones.

Among the metasystem's output parameters is a key factor: the management of shared resources devoted to learning, also 'vis-à-vis' other investments.

In an organization, some processes create more ROI than average, while others use it up. Planning and budgeting are crucial processes that the metasystem needs to influence, *allocating capital to seek higher returns on learning.*

Graphically, in relation to the parasystems, it is useful to visualize the metasystem sitting at the core. Multiple parasystems support the organization's core processes by monitoring performance and environment, and then giving feedback to the central metasystem.

It can focus on improving an existing parasystem or change the rules to encourage more innovative learning.

We can see it also as an *'organizational consciousness'* that interrogates the learning objectives. The prefix 'meta' suggests a higher level of awareness, like 'metathinking,' which means thinking about how you think.

And that is what a well-designed learning metasystem does:

- identifies parasystemic learning gaps and performance
- review learning investment allocations and their return
- triggers structural modifications, *if tension has built up*
- in extreme cases, they can redirect or assume control

THE COLLECTIVE LEARNING SYSTEM

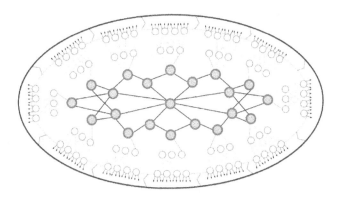

THE BRAIN OF THE ORGANIZATION

Stafford Beer[3] pioneered an organizational model likened to a biological system. His brilliance lies in the analogies he drew between the functions of the human nervous system and that of organizational structures.

When he spoke of the 'brain,' he referred to those instances requiring high-level conscious decision-making. Other less complex but more frequent matters are left to the organization's 'autonomic nervous system.'

Yet, it is important to note that Beer's focus was not on understanding the learning process.

He was not concerned with how, under repeated stimulus, responses begin to become 'unconscious.' *Nor did he explore the design of an organizational 'brain' or 'spinal cord'.*

His main aim was to create a model comparing an organization to the human body's control system.

For us, the focus is on understanding the phenomenon of organizational learning. We have an advantage that Beer did not at the time: *remarkable progress in the understanding of natural neural networks.*

The brain today is more than just an unexplained processor of conscious thoughts. *It's a complex structure of neurons, simple cells layered in complex ways, yet able to distill abstraction.*

The closer the neurons are to the nerves, the more they process sensory information, extracting basic patterns, processing them, and passing the outputs onto the subsequent layers.

Moreover, brain studies show functional specialization, reinforcing the validity of the framework proposed:

- neurons responsible for vision are different from those responsible for other sensorial inputs, like sound
- memories are not stored in the neurons themselves but in the synaptic interconnections between them
- there are areas shaped by 'supervised learning,' based-on feedback, like when a child learns to read

- however, in most instances, other areas display the ability to learn without any supervision

Given this, there is a tremendous potential in aligning the structure of a learning organization with our understanding biological *(collective)* structure capable of learning: the brain.

***

As for networks of information *'canali'*, in the case of the organizational brain, these are far away from being an optical illusion or a construct of imagination.

We will explore next the cybernetic research behind the learning capabilities of information arrays, *where simple, yet very interconnected, nodes provide foundational proof to the collective learning paradigm.* The field of Artificial Neural Networks.

8

NEURAL NETWORKS
A New Paradigm of Collective Learning

W E WILL DISCUSS MODELLING organizational learning structures based on the latest findings in artificial neural networks, *computational structures that operating solely on collective learning.* These networks, able to learn to recognize images and speech without writing a single line of code, solely by training on simulated computational arrays, can be used to conceptualize organizational parasystemic and metasystemic learning systems. In general, this approach has two advantages:

1. Neural Networks are easy to understand and represent, *making them suitable for illustrating organizational analogies,* and

2. Simulations of a learning model can be run on a computer to examine its problem-solving behavior *(whether it converges easily, or conversely, explore why it becomes unstable)*

THE QUEST FOR HOW THE BRAIN WORKS

Before we get started, to help root our thinking, let's reflect on the first *meta thinkers,* philosophers hypothesizing how is that we learn and adapt, leading to the birth of modern neurology, *and how it came to influence the artificial neural network discipline.*

This will help set the context for the neural models that can help us reflect the properties of collective learning that apply for parasystems and metasystems.

Aristoteles: The Heart as the Center of Thinking and the brain as a cooling device...

The problem addressed by scholars of neural networks is not new. Over 2,500 years ago, Pre-Socratic philosophers and ancient doctors were formulating tentative hypotheses about the relationship between the brain and the origins of our perceptions, thoughts, and actions. Among others:

- *Alcmaeon of Croton (6 BC), is the first on record proposing the brain as the center of intelligence*

- *Plato (4 BC)* supported those views, often quoting that *'the brain is the organ of reason'*

- *Hippocrates (4 BC) and Galen (2 BC)* quoted Alcmaeon, *spousing all ideas stem from the brain*

- *Twenty centuries later, Leonardo, 'Renaissance Man,'* dissecting bodies to seek answers, said *'the brain is the interpreter for the other members'*

'Alcmaeon believed the nerves are the channels through
which information travels between the brain and the body'
- GALEN[1]

But Aristoteles, had a different opinion. *The heart, and not*
the brain, is where all ideas emanate from. Aristoteles probably
was the best communicator of ancient times, maybe of all
history. *He thrived on the power of his oratory and crisp*
explanations.

It is remarkable that his legacy, *brilliant when it comes to*
human values, thrived through time despite multiple wrong
theories, brain function included, setting back science for a
long while.

'ARISTOTELES' SCIENTIFIC HOAXES[2]

topic	aristotelian theory	real paradigm	scientist
Spontaneous Generation	Life arises spontaneously from non-living matter	Life arises from pre-existing life	Pasteur
Forced Motion Theory	Motion is a forced state, until reaching 'natural rest'	Objects in motion stay in motion	Newton
Geocentricity	Earth is at the universe's center, all bodies revolving around it	The sun is our solar system center	Copernicus, Kepler, Galileo
The Brain is a Cooling Device	It cools the blood, not involved in thinking (the heart does)	The brain is the center of cognition	Ramon y Cajal

Every kid learns today how those myths were dispelled.
Pasteur took on spontaneous generation, Newton set the
motion record straight.

Geocentricity was a bit more dramatic, with Sagan's
blockbuster Cosmos reminding us of that journey.

Giants like Copernicus, Kepler and Galileo put their lives on the line to defy that paradigm. Heliocentricity finally triumphed in the early 1700s. *But it took another two centuries for Aristoteles' brain theories to be challenged.*

> *'The heart is the origin of the senses and of though. The brain is unimportant, the coldest part of all animals'*
> *- ARISTOTLE*

For two millennia, we kept his brain beliefs, 'following our hearts'. An expression still alive in language. A fascinating, untold story.

As telescopes aimed for the skies, Jansen's microscope, with the likes of Leeuwenhoek at the aperture, were finding every single cell across all organs, revealing their structure.

All but one, where no microscope would discern any cells: *The brain.*

As soon that it became obvious that our hearts just pump blood, conveniently the intellect moved back *(no controversy or heresy trials here)* to the one 'unexplainable' organ: *the brain:*

- *A convenient repository for the 'soul', composed of unexplained 'grey matter' (von Sömmerring, 1791)* [3]

- *The only organ with no observable cells, just fibers, originating the 'reticular theory' (Golgi, 1870)* [4]

Brain and nerve tissue fused like a closed-loop, filament network. People were quick to propose theories, seeking 'organs'...

THE PROLIFERATION OF BRAIN PSEUDOSCIENCE[5]

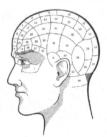

Gall's Phrenology main tenets (1810):

- *shape of skull reflects personality*
- *localization of function*
- *organology - benevolence, secretiveness, destructiveness supported by organoids*
- *measurable skull features reveal character*
- *innate traits determined at birth*

Biological Neural Networks: The Birth of Neuroscience

However, in Spain, Santiago Ramón y Cajal was about to change everything, and be awarded a Nobel in the process. He became the first person to observe the building blocks of the brain, their connectivity, and interactions: *the neurons.*

This milestone was possible, as the story goes, by an epiphany Don Santiago's had at the kitchen table while having breakfast: [6]

- *As his beloved daughter, Silveria, then a toddler was having a tantrum, he comforted the family: 'as she grows up, her brain will develop, she will learn to manage her temperament...'*

- *Reportedly, as he said these words, he realized why he and all his colleagues around the world had been failing: all the samples analyzed belonged to adult specimens...*

- *What if the connections grow so quickly that they hide the cells? What if these cells do not die, and instead the brain just gains complexity as these 'fibers' somehow keep growing?*

- *The rest is history: rushing to the lab, leaving his coffee behind, he took a sample of a chick embryo and was the first person alive to see a neuron.*

His scientific drawings, exquisite works of art, documenting in detail this most elusive, highly specialized cell.

The nucleus pales in comparison to the ramifications (particularly the input ones, named by him as 'dendrites') and prior-seen 'long fibers' (axons), acting as outputs.

This milestone marked the birth of a new scientific discipline, *neurology, dedicated to studying brain function.*

The identification of the neuron's dendrites revealed woven layers with thousands of input and output connections.

Over time, major focus has shifted to their connectivity and ability to process and propagate electrical stimuli.

HOW BIOLOGICAL NEURONS WORK

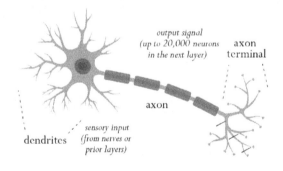

The field evolved into several major disciplines, including:

1) *Neurophysiology:* Studies the properties of neurons, synapses, and circuits, *measuring electrical and chemical activity to understand how neurons process information*

2) *Cognitive neuroscience:* Explores support to psychological cognitive process *to understand how brain function correlates with perception, memory, language, and decision-making*

3) *Systems neurobiology:* Examines how groups of neurons form functional networks to control systems like *sensory, motor, and the limbic abilities.*

A hundred years later, the results might seem discouraging at first glance. Despite significant advances in understanding the neural structure of the brain, the connection between this structure, its neural network *(nerve tissue),* and perceptual-cognitive abilities remains somewhat an early *work-in-progress.*

The main difficulty lies in the complexities, non-linearities, and parallel organization of the brain.

Artificial Neural Networks: The Emerging Paradigm

Paradoxically, the complexity of solving this problem attracted scientists from many disciplines:

- *Neurologists and biologists* obviously continued efforts to model the functioning of natural neural networks in the brains of humans via electro encephalograms (ECG) and researching in-depth animal models

- *Physicists and systems engineers* began avidly reading these research findings, establishing analogies between the dynamic behavior of brain systems and non-linear dynamic systems familiar in physics

- *Mathematicians, particularly logicians and network theoreticians,* searching for ways to model the learning process – either through logic or structural simulation

- *Electronic and computer engineers and scientists,* saw the potential to apply this structural knowledge to build computers with Central Processing Units (CPUs), inspired by known brain structures

So who 'programs' the brain? Neurologists were not able to discern any set 'learning programs' in the brain.

It was a self-organizing structure, whose configuration changed based on exposure to different situations.

'Cells That Fire Together, Wire Together' - *DONALD HEBB*

It's unnecessary to elaborate on the interest these hypotheses generated across the other fields, and they set to the task of proving that self-organizing networks of simple 'artificial neurons' could learn.

What human brains are to Neuroscience, artificial neural networks became to Computational Neuroscience.

And as Neurobiology has a founding father, this new field came to have a few of them:

KEY COMPUTATIONAL NEUROSCIENTISTS 1943-93

yr	contribution	researcher	research center
43	*Developed the first conceptual proposal for an artificial neuron*	McCulloch & Pitts[7]	University of Illinois
49	*Introduced Hebbian learning in "The Organization of Behavior"*	Donald Hebb[8]	McGill University
56	*Coined the term 'AI', developed LISP language*	John McCarthy[9]	Dartmouth College and Stanford University
57	*Created the Perceptron, first layered neural network*	Frank Rosenblatt[10]	Cornell University
65	*Proposed algorithms supporting multi-layered networks*	Ivakhnenko & Lapa[11]	Kyiv Institute of Cybernetics
70	*Perceptron Critique... Neural Network 'Nuclear Winter'*	Minsky & Papert[12]	Massachusetts Institute of Technology
80	*Developed the Neocognitron, a hierarchical, multilayered NN*	Kunihiko Fukushima[13]	Osaka University
82	*Self-organizing map (SOM), a type of artificial neural network*	Teuvo Kohonen[14]	Helsinki University of Technology
86	*Pioneered work in deep learning and backpropagation in neural networks*	Geoffrey Hinton[15]	University of Toronto
89	*First Convolutional Neural Network, handwriting processing*	Yann LeCun[16]	New York University

Notably, McCulloch & Pitts[7] *developed the first proposal for an artificial neuron in 1943,* Donald Hebb[8] *came with the learning component in 1949* and Frank Rosenblatt[10], who brought the first array of a networked, single layer of artificial neurons in 1957.

The promise of this intriguing technology attracted leading mathematicians around the world, Ivakhnenko and Lapa[11] proposing, as early as 1965, the first multi-layer neural array.

By 1956, the term Artificial Intelligence was being coined by McCarthy[9], and leading academics across all emergent AI disciplines *(Neural Networks, Symbolic AI...)* started a new field.

However, no theoretical field progresses without detractors. Minsky and Papert's[12] (fair) critique of the Perceptron Model, *the first single-layer network,* unable to perform a XOR logical function, sent the field into a 'nuclear winter' for years. Symbolic logicians would propose languages such as LISP and Prolog, while funding for neural networks became scarce.

Fortunately in the 80's, computational processing power enabled larger models: Fukushima's[13] advanced work in the *Neocognitron* would allow for recognition of complex kanji ideograms, and the field experimented a huge comeback.

Learning could be both supervised and unsupervised *(Kohonen, 82)*[14], and with increased sophistication, neural networks displayed amazing plasticity, *able to perform very complex tasks such as handwritten recognition (LeCun, 89)* [16].

The potential of these developments are immense. *What if circuits were designed emulating known neural structures as well as the basic aspects of their dynamic behavior?* Would it be possible to build machines with the intelligence of biological organisms?

Their success is surprising even the most skeptical critics. Neural network implementations are capable of performing functions such as image recognition, processing language, making statistical predictions, and intuitively solving optimization problems. *All of this being achieved without writing a single line of code about how the network should solve the problem.*

It is necessary to clarify, for the non-technical audience, *that just the simulations of neural networks needs to be programmed,* since today they lack a hardware representation; *no CPU or microchip has been designed that can support that level of connectivity.* However, what is coded is only the representation of the simulated network elements and the learning algorithm.

Neural Network Models in Organization Theory

We believe there is a remarkable applicability of neural networks as a modeling tool in organizational learning is driven by two main characteristics:

1. It doesn't rely on any algorithmically expressed rationalization to explain learning, and
2. It explains complex forms of collective learning array from a structural point of view, superseding the capabilities of its processing elements

However, it's worth noting that the prolific developments in the area of neural networks have generated an enormous variety of basic networks.

These range from the precursor perceptron, comprised of 'binary' artificial neurons with no intermediate values, to the far more evolved *Neo-Cognitron* by Fukushima, used for Kanji character recognition.

Significant work would be required to perform a mathematical representation of a social collective *(well beyond the scope of the present work)*, where the processing entities at each layer could have different processing capabilities and wired in hybrid manners.

However, there are many structural variations emerging, *from which we can draw inspiration from,* depicting the ability of collective learning to occur under a wide set of premises:

- Types of neurons *(transfer functions)*,
- Neuron's thresholds *(continuous or binary output)*
- Network's topology *(how neurons are wired)*
- Network's density *(neurons per layer, number of layers)*
- Feedback parameters *(learning / forgetfulness rates)*
- Supervised learning *(with varying algorithms),* or
- Unsupervised learning (dynamically feedback-driven or controlled networks, self-organizing maps…)
- And many others…

Therefore, when it comes to proposing structural neural network examples for modeling the collective behavior of both learning parasystems and metasystems, the options are diverse.

PARASYSTEMIC NEURAL MODELS

To model the basic qualities of learning parasystems, basic models should suffice, *based on versions of Hebbian learning:*

- These networks, characterized by *'supervised learning,'* rely on monitored feeding of training data sets

- Computationally, the simplest network required for visualization would be a *multi-layer perceptron network,* a 'feed-forward' neural network, able to differentiate multiple features *(more complex models would do as well)*
- to simulate reinforcement of consequences, we can use Rumelhart's[15] 1986 backpropagation algorithm, *able to illustrate the properties of this level of collective learning*

Qualitatively, this learning algorithm aligns with how the nodes *(neurons)* in the learning parasystem reinforce the learning connections that produce successful responses:

- Training datasets are backpropagated to the input neurons, *output differences are analyzed vs. expected*
- Gains *(signal amplification coefficients)* from inputs that led to successful responses are positively reinforced, *and those that led to failed decisions are reduced.*
- *The balance between these input gains vs. the supervisor's feedback will determine the network's rate of forgetting*

In this analogy, parasystemic teams, layered around core processes extract features from successful and unsuccessful responses. *The resulting analytical groups self-organize in relevant features for the process, based on data (not dictated from the top).*

METASYSTEMIC NEURAL MODELS

While parasystemic networks and their learning algorithm are relatively easy to understand, they have a practical limitation: *they requires a 'supervisor' to monitor the successful training and operation of the learning subsystem vis-à-vis its goal tree.*

In our proposed framework, parasystemic teams across the organization are regulated and evaluated by a metasystem. However, a logical question arises: *who trains the meta-system?*

Fortunately, the low biological likelihood that an important proportion of *'natural neural learning'* would be supervised, led scientists in the field to deeply explore this topic.

In doing so, self-organizing maps and dynamic feedback-driven models where researched, *these converge towards the solution without the previously described backpropagation algorithm.*

The nature of their operation relies in the propagation of the constraints associated with all the inputs *(i.e. in a world with limited resources, how much we could invest improving training datasets or parasystems, given realistic return expectations).*

Two basic alternatives exist today, with different use cases:

1) Kohonen's Self-Organizing maps, great to extract map features, *enabling the visualization of complex datasets,* and

2) Hopfield Networks, a type of recurrent neural network, where the output is feedback to the input, *result in a kind of associative memory, able to solve complex problems such as the 'Travelling Salesman Problem' without training*

Without engaging in a formal technical discussion to extensively compare the merits of both, the use of Hopfield's[15] developments is recommended.

These remarkable networks, proposed in 1982 by Hopfield[17] at Caltech, *use the concept of energy to converge to a solution, as they naturally seek stability by minimizing their 'energy' function.*

Its intuitive operation perfectly fits how the learning meta-system appears to operate. This utility stems from the fact that the Hopfield network feeds its outputs back into its inputs, allowing it to solve constraint propagation and optimization problems around a specific energy function.

And this is exactly where the effort needs to be placed for the metasystem: the definition of an energy function where all the optimization variables discussed *(learning offer intensity, mix, costs of 'G' and 'M' factors and problem intensity comes into play).*

Intuitively, the network learns by seeking a configuration that minimizes the network's energy function.

Interestingly, the notion of feeding the output of the process back into the input may seem trivial to those familiar with Organization Theory. While this is strictly true for well-defined systems *(linear or non-linear), stability in a distributed system is much more complex.* System Dynamics made this a popular concept in Organization Theory, mistakenly commingling the concept of *'solving a process problem'* with representing how to *'collectively learn about how to solve problems.'*

In the early days of Neural Networks, complex, multilayered networks were very unstable when taking 'live output' feedback. It wasn't until 1983 that Cohen and Grossberg[18] made developments that allowed for stability in certain configurations of Hopfield networks.

The interesting aspect of these networks is the collective behavior of these neurons. The system can solve complicated optimization problems given the defined energy landscape

So, there is a relationship between how the metasystem operates to 'release' its potential energy, in the process to solve for complex optimization. *This is a most important and clear analogy for traditional designers venturing into the realm of designing intelligent organizations.*

The work to model these networks is not easy, requiring skills in computer science and mathematics to set up the simulation environments and configure the network topology. However, specialized tools are emerging that facilitate this task and can help us explore the dynamics of self-learning arrays.

***

The potential to apply both types of neural models to the modeling of collective learning systems is immense. A traditionally *'soft'* area considered *'non modellable,'* could now be computationally simulated by adapting these structural neural paradigms – and address *'hard'* inference along the way.

9

INSTRUMENTING FOUNDATIONAL DESIGN

Fostering Generative Learning Structures

I NSTRUMENTING THE DESIGN of the learning organization is the next step in our stage-by-stage transformation methodology. This phase addresses clear-cut strategies to handle design parameters, with the intent of bringing pivotal enhancements to the learning system.

Consistent with established design conventions, we will explore ways in which various design elements shape the learning system's dynamics.

Through the remaining chapters, we will propose recommendations to enhance learning, centering on the *design of positions, overarching structures, planning & control methods, communication channels, and decision-making processes.*

A fairly straightforward process in traditional design, positions are set on a static skill view, documented processes are available, used both in training and value discussions.

TYPICAL ORGANIZATIONAL REPRESENTATIONS

This chapter will focus on the basic aspects of organization design, from the ground up: Positions, Processes and Training.

- *Position Design:* In learning organizations, encompassing the range from generative roles to specialized positions
- *Work Process Formalization:* Depicted as a double-edge sword – on one side, it preserves memory, while on the other, it may hamper the integration of fresh learnings
- *Training and Indoctrination:* This involves both the learning skills and values guiding the learning journey

INSTRUMENTING DESIGN FOR LEARNING

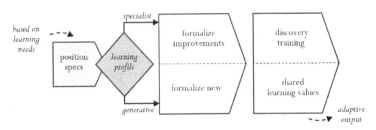

PIVOTAL POSITION DESIGN

LAYING THE FOUNDATIONS FOR SYSTEMIC LEARNING

Historically, we have seen position specifications that just enumerate tasks of varying complexity. Rarely those would incorporate the ability to learn as a requirement:

- Prior experience in the area, ideally with education aligned within the same discipline

- Familiarity with processes and standards, as well as regulations

- Ability to communicate with the expected stakeholders in the industry for that type of function

- Familiarity with the geographies, languages, or similar organizational cultures

- Professional certifications and working knowledge of some software applications

However, this approach is geared towards execution: often the candidates fitting better these specifications would be the ones that most tenured within one track have depicted familiarity with rules, set regulations and standards and seek to perform within those boundaries.

In the learning organization, the ability to observe new patterns, innovate within your track or see new opportunities is critical. We will examine how to affect job design, in order to impact an organization's collective learning.

LEARNING JOB SPECIALIZATION

The first task at hand is to characterize learning needs. How does the number, nature and specialization of tasks affect learning? Is high throughput expected highly repetitive tasks, or the addressing a small amount of very complex problems?

Senge offers an interesting perspective. A key point affecting an organization's learning is its members' ability to develop systemic thinking. *That organizational 'metathinking', thinking about individual and collective thinking,* is an intriguing attribute.

A concern under this approach is where to source this systemic thinking profile. This ability demands an outstanding mental discipline, complemented by very specific skills:

SYSTEMIC THINKING QUALITIES

individual	attribute	collective
cognitive recognition	*self-awareness*	*team introspection*
analyzing thoughts	*reflection*	*collaborative analysis*
rigorous evaluation	*critical thinking*	*collective reasoning*
open-mindedness	*cognitive flexibility*	*team adaptability*
future challenges	*strategic planning*	*collaborative strategy*

A difficult requirement to fulfill, hence rarely defined. Unless the business ecosystem thrives with systemic learning practices *(as it is probably the case in today's Japanese economy),* resourcing systemic thinkers may prove to be a hard endeavor.

THE ILLUSION OF BALANCED LEARNING

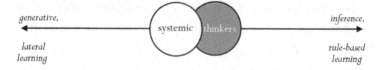

We made this remark earlier on. The realities of staffing a 'systems design' office are grueling. Yet many companies insist on staffing transformation offices, prone to lose traction.

Characterizing the Position Learning Profile

However, it may be possible to characterize learning types, when designing learning positions *(and subsequently recruiting for them)*. *For that, it is useful to assess the expected level of vertical and horizontal engagement,* when it comes to problem-solving.

REALITY: UNBALANCED LEARNING TYPES

horizontal engagement	attribute	vertical engagement
broad across disciplines	knowledge breadth	narrow & deep, one field
interdisciplinary	learning approach	specialized
integrates across fields	knowledge application	masters one domain
adapts & connects ideas	flexibility	refines & perfects ideas
diverse teams & topics	collaboration preference	experts in the same area

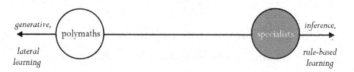

As individuals perform a broader variety of tasks *(horizontal role expansion)*, they gain generativity – having to adapt learning patterns to new situations, becoming polymaths at different aspects of the operation, gaining a broader view.

Conversely, increasing vertical expansion, can help individuals control more aspects of their work in the same area, gain a deeper, yet narrower, more specialized experience. The path of a specialist, versed in all the aspects of the trade, more prone to deep dive into incremental improvements than adding value to the 'big picture', or connecting dots across the org.

There is no right or wrong type of learning, we actually need both to support a multifaceted learning frontier, as collectives solve all types of strategic and operational problems to succeed. In essence, the learning frontier of the organization needs to display a wide array of groupings, some more generative, some more rule-inference oriented.

VARYING MIX OF LEARNING TYPES WITHIN AN ORG

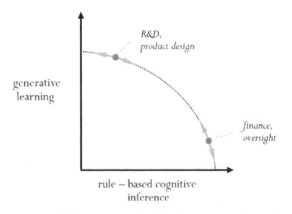

This view starkly contrasts with the approach traditionally favored by designers, which emphasizes job specialization to limit variability and discretion in activities, aiming to benefit from short-term gains that come from 'proven' specialization.

However, these gains come at a cost: excessive specialization can yield many long-term side effects such as organizational stagnation, inflexibility, demotivation, and communication gaps. *Over time, these costs eclipse the envisioned short-term gains.*

In contrast, learning designers see the system as a whole, making explicit the costs of overspecialization. Mixing diverse learning types, cross-pollinating experts outside their zones of comfort can yield outstanding collective learning results.

Examples abound in the military realm, where armies, the ultimate formal hierarchical orgs, seek major innovations, often at the brink of collapse, by short-circuiting dusting expert networks. Look at the Manhattan Project[1]:

FINDING EQUILIBRIUM: THE MANHATTAN PROJECT

The potential immense benefits of increasing horizontal specialization in an organization are often overlooked. Properly applied, it can reshape the collective learning curve, in particular when the ability to innovate is diminished due to the overspecialization across the organization, or the industry.

We are not arguing that specialization is not critical for competitiveness. The Manhattan project would not be possible without the deep experts involved.

Yet, the prior absence of polymaths aligned with the realities of the field, had held back the learning process, hampering progress towards a critical military competency required to end WWII. There is more to that historic learning catalyzation, but undeniably the addition of polymaths like Oppenheimer and many others like Fermi and Von Neumann, carried the other intellectual giants

So, from a learning design perspective, it's possible to foster systemic thinking through multidisciplinary teams:

- The right mix of learning types and skill depth

- Aligned supporting processes, systems, and incentives

- Flexible mechanisms of coordination and control

This multidisciplinary team of specialists thus attains a more comprehensive view of the system than any of its individual members could achieve on their own.

But how do we create expertise of different types? *How do we foster extraordinary role learning when we are not Caltech, and not that many Nobel Prizes are lining up to fulfill our open positions?*

Position Learning Framework in the Neural Paradigm

In our learning model, *'on the job' specialization correlates with the dimensionality of the input vector of the parasystemic neurons (breadth), which serve as a proxy for pattern identification complexity and the overall structure (depth) of the network.*

Both dimensions affect *the individual processors (neurons) to be selected in each layer, their position and evolution through time.*

Breadth: Dimensionality and Complexity

Imagine for a moment a first-layer neuron equivalent to a position role, the more numerous and diverse its input connections, *the greater the horizontal expansion of that position.*

- The amplification of the 'fan' of inputs, with high variability enhances generative capabilities

- Conversely, if the processor element is connected to a poor set of input variables with little variation over time, the generation of alternatives is severely affected

There's a clear structural relationship between parasystemic learning generativity and the number of relevant input connections associated with each neuron or processing role.

Not only is the number of input connections crucial, but also their flexibility to change their configuration or weighting over time. *This discretion underpins the network's self-organizing capacity, the foundation of adaptive learning.*

In our model, such changes are catalyzed by the selective tension applied by the metasystem. However, the lower the potential required for change *(lower organizational resistance to the readjustment of horizontal dimensioning of jobs),* the more effective the control process will be.

HORIZONTAL LEARNING: THE PERCEPTRON MODEL

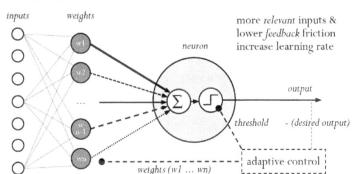

So, the differences between the desired output and the output activate 'adaptive control' mechanisms:

- The weight of the input variables *(think about it as attention),* and
- The transfer function *(in this case a simple summation and threshold function, to trigger or not a simple action)*

This type of control is akin to the one known in cybernetics as 'adaptive control' and was first applied in artificial neural networks when engineering the perceptron model.

Depth: Featurization and Memory

The other key variable suggested involves vertically broadening the position.

In the neural paradigm, the structural implication of this measure involves linking the output value of the neuron, through multiple layers, *extracting specialized features*, with the procedure under observation.

This is critical for the learning algorithm of the network to converge: The higher the correlation between the elements of the input vector and the observability of the desired consequences of its response on the process, the greater the learning convergence will be.

VERTICAL LEARNING: STACKING LAYERS

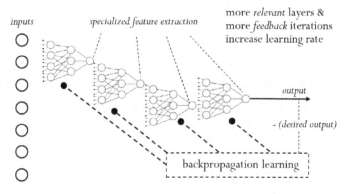

Adaptation times for the coefficients will be shorter, and thus, the network's problem-solving ability improves.

Balancing Position Learning in the Neural Paradigm

So, there are ways to increase learning breadth in the positions and empower their ability to make connections across an array of very different variables. On the other hand, we can also encourage highly focused arrays, narrowing down scope and specializing learning units to extract specific features, iterating multiple times to hone very specific knowledge.

At the end, under the neural paradigm, with a base of cases of success and failure, the system is configured *(neuronal models, span of connections, depth of the network)*, much as we would combine experts and polymaths roles on a team. And a key feature that is sought after is *the stability of the network: Its ability to converge through iterations to an optimal learning point.*

COLLECTIVE LEARNING: THE QUEST FOR CONVERGENCE

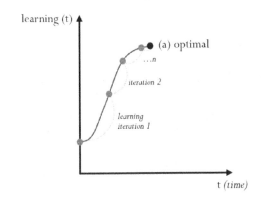

The stability of the learning network is a critical, yet elusive point, often overlooked.

The initial aim is to establish a system that will consistently distill insights and converge into a paradigm, while being able to address some levels of increased complexity.

If stability is not achieved, everything else is in vain. Only after assessing whether we have a viable learning array, we seek to optimize the speed and quality of collective learning.

Where do the design trade-offs lie? What is the cost of the options to stabilize and optimize learning? Both horizontal and vertical broadening have their practical limitations.

AVOIDING COLLECTIVE LEARNING MISHAPS

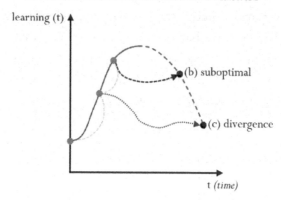

The reality imposed by more complex problems, reaching a collective learning array that remains untouched, results in learning degradation. *Training optimization can only do so much to increase the learning frontier.*

In general, periodically reassessing learning positions and their configuration needs to become a core organizational rhythm of the learning organization. It should be really a cursory part of business, since it is a critical attribute for learning organizations.

Even the best *one-off* designs balancing horizontal connectivity *(often conducive to more generativity)* and vertical learning *(associated with perfecting existing heuristics),* need to be subject to regular performance measurements *vis-à-vis* the evolution of the problem space. As an example:

-   Brand-new variables *(features, products, markets)* dilutes the value added by prior specialized learning 'transfer functions,' requiring an assessment
    Added horizontal role connectivity may be needed in such cases

- Conversely, the same input vector could show increased variance *(typical of a sector facing more competitive intensity)*

  Increased focus to address input complexity may be required, adding additional specialization to those roles upfront

In conclusion, striking the right balance is crucial. Any perceived sacrifice of generativity or specialization at the individual unit level should be addressed through higher level groupings *(to be explored in a subsequent section)*.

Next, we will focus on the degree of formalization, or the extent to which roles and tasks are standardized and documented, which can have profound implications on an organization's ability to learn and adapt.

FORMALIZATION

Should the learning organization encourage highly standardized work processes? At first glance, formalized routines would limit individual discretion, appearing to seriously hinder experimentation and communication processes essential for learning.

PERCEPTION:
FORMALIZATION LIMITS LEARNING

However, this apparent truism may only hold on the surface. Paradoxically, formalization is indeed necessary for learning:

- *Formalization transforms past learnings into routines,* thus becoming the fundamental mechanism for organizational memory

- *In the ideal state, this organizational memory would be relational,* where changes to the formalized processed are related to the situations triggering the modifications

- An additional learning value is when the learnings from documented *cause-and-effect* patterns can be extrapolated to other process contexts, through time.

Formalization Duality

The potential duality of the value of formalization to learning processes *(as an apparent deterrent, yet key to enable memory processes)*, makes it a challenging parameter to manage.

It seems necessary to develop a new formalization schema, which could be termed *'Adaptive Formalization.'*

REALITY:
ADAPTIVE FORMALIZATION ENABLES LEARNING

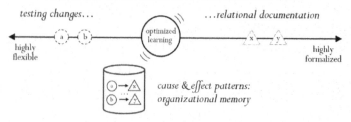

This seemingly contradictory term would describe formalization systems capable of preserving organizational learning *(memory)*, without limiting the necessary flexibility to enrich established routines.

Adaptive Formalization in the Neural Learning Model

In the neural learning model, adaptive formalization is akin to the parasystem's *learning algorithm, which commands both 'set process' reinforcements and the forgetting rate of the network.*

As we have discussed. once information is processed by each learning unit *(neurons)* and their aggregated outputs affects the process, feedback regarding the appropriateness of the action taken will be used to modify input weights: positive reinforcement if successful, negative if not.

The higher the weights variance, the greater the *'forgetting rate'* of the network. In the organizational equivalent, these weights are perceptual filters formed through norms and procedures. *The laxer the norms, the higher generative learning, at the expense of a higher forgetting rate.*

Implications of Formalization

Greater formalization directly impacts the cognitive inference capacity of the network. Strict adherence to rules will favor learning based on past rules and norms, limiting generativity but favoring consistency with past learning outcomes.

On the other hand, very low formalization increases the rate of forgetting; responses will mostly be influenced by recent learnings – maybe only fitting highly volatile situations.

While formalization standardizes processes reflecting past learnings, training and indoctrination seek to equip organizational members with the skills necessary for both preserving and adapting to new knowledge as well.

Let's focus next on how *training and indoctrination* further affect the learning dynamics within an organization.

TRAINING AND INDOCTRINATION

What influence does the formal standardization and dissemination of organizational knowledge and culture have on learning levels? An interesting view, recently espoused by Nelson and Winter[2] (1982), makes the case that organizations can be seen as a repertoire of skills.

From this viewpoint, organizational learning takes the form of a process that contributes to building and modifying this repertoire. Training programs aimed at supporting the development of organizational members will then have a positive effect on this set of skills.

Common Flaws in Traditional Training Approaches

However, most traditional training programs suffer from common flaws: Questions about the effectiveness, relevance, and practical applicability of training systems are common topics of discussion in many organizations

- In some companies, courses are viewed as *rewards for good performance,* and 'extra padding' *(e.g., exotic locations)* create potential distortions

- In other cases, excessive planning and articulation make training more about fulfilling a schedule on a weekly basis, checking a box more than meeting learning needs

Keys for Effective Training Programs

The designer of the learning organization must recognize that effective training programs hinge on:

1) Flexibility: Providing key individuals with the autonomy to tailor their training within the boundaries of

   - their own direct information processing needs

   - the role they fulfill in the collective learning process

2) Immediate or Near-Term Applicability: Ensuring prompt real-world utilization of the gained knowledge.

3) Accountability to show the value of training should be rewarded, in terms of visibility, revised charter or even responsibilities to propagate the acquired knowledge.
   - honest evaluation of utility, *reward failure if needed*
   - extension to similar candidates *(learning roles exposed to equivalent challenges)*

4) Training programs should be conceived and managed as *a 'product to end customers.'* It is key to avoid the pitfall of treating it as a *'merit good'*, force-fed to participants.

By focusing on these elements, the organization not only empowers its members but also promotes a culture of proactive learning, proven skill mastery and application.

Such an approach transcends traditional approaches, curbs skills 'memory loss' and becomes a tool for growth and improvement, enabling collective *'just-in-time-knowledge'*

Structural Representation of the Neural Learning Training

Under the neural paradigm, it is quite straightforward to represent training on the structural model of the organizational learning system: It is reflected in the connections and transfer functions of each processing element in the network.

Every neuron in the learning network *(both parasystemic and metasystemic)* combines weighted input vector values to produce an output, by means of a transfer function, that will feed second-level processing units.

Through training, it's possible to increase the capacity of this system to learn, by:

- *Augmenting the number of processing units in the input layers,*
- *Adjust the transfer functions conforming the range of variance expected that each layer can feed forward*

In Shannon's[3] language, the lead academic of Information Theory, *it's about balancing the number of input channels, each one with its corresponding bandwidth, with the information processing capacity of the learning system transfer function.*

So, through training, you're not just impacting the capacity of a function, but its effective shape and bandwidth as well.

Imagine your organization as a complex neural network being calibrated; an updated training dataset effectively acts like a well-timed algorithmic adjustment, triggering changes that can enhance overall organizational performance.

Traditional *vs.* Learning Indoctrination

Traditional indoctrination aims to create systems of 'values', aligning the individual with a set of corporate loyalties *(to duty, teams, and the responsibility associated with their outcomes).*

However, in a learning organization, the indoctrination tone *should strengthen the individual self-affirmation of learning values to embrace collective change, as opposed to a static status quo.*

Loyalty to learning values starts by reinforcing the individual learning ideals and the responsibility to extend them to their team. Practically speaking there two key aspects:

- *A commitment to truth:* embracing fact-based objectivity as an explicit value. It becomes an 'anti-filter', adding transparency and delayering perceptual processes
- *An unwavering promise for continuous improvement:* staying committed to enhanced organizational learning, by:
    - encouraging a learning culture at all levels,
    - promoting cultural values that lead to more effective communication of knowledge, and
    - enabling the learning of working teams: the duty to share knowledge: *Communicational Indoctrination*

A way to visualize indoctrination's effects in the neural paradigm *is as a Hopfield network's energy function.* These hyper-connected networks *(all neurons are connected directly)* stabilize efficiently, converging with fewer iterations *(training energy).* *Learning Indoctrination aims for that stable, efficient learning state.*

Summative Hypotheses

In summary, when designing roles within a learning organization, several hypotheses emerge:

1. *Designing learning positions, addressing the mix of horizontal or vertical specialization* to configure learning profiles,
2. *Adaptive formalization: process changes & causality,*
3. *Training maximizing 'Just-In-Time Knowledge,'* and
4. *Learning Indoctrination* to catalyze learning

Industries fierce competition will rapidly evolve learning positions to master the challenge. *Take McLaren's F1 example[4].*

MCLAREN: EVOLUTION OF ROLES OVER 20 YEARS

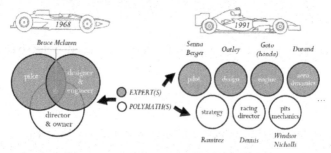

1968	attribute	1991
undifferentiated	1. learning positions	highly differentiated
technical manuals	2. adaptive formalization	tailored causal routines
ad hoc, on-the-seat	3. training	simulators, attention span
individual risks, guts	4. indoctrination	telemetry, metrics-driven

Like an F1 team, as complexity increases, a single entity *(even as gifted as Bruce McLaren)*, cannot handle it all.

By balancing these parameters *(learning role design, adaptive formalization, JIT training, and learning indoctrination)*, the 'Learning-Designability' curve can be affected. This will result in adjusting both the learning types and the curve's shape, augmenting the learning plays available to the organization.

THE LEARNING-DESIGNABILITY CURVE

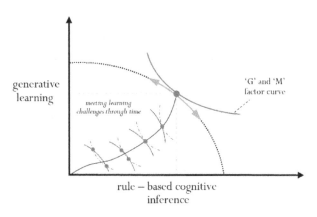

These aren't just academic ideas; they are levers leaders can pull to make teams more adaptive.

***

But while these levers can make a Formula 1 team thrive, what about enhancing the whole Grand Prix Ecosystem? That is the focus of the Learning Superstructure.

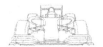

10

DESIGNING THE LEARNING SUPERSTRUCTURE

Crafting collective learning

S UPERSTRUCTURES. Beyond the operational base, all organizations have a 'superstructure', which whether explicitly or implicitly, holds the organization's values, culture, and corporate governance. The superstructure then, is the backbone where operations are configured, functional responsibilities established and critical processes such as corporate planning, control and key decisions are made.

The superstructure exerts great impact on the collective learning capacity. The reporting structure of the organization, the criteria for grouping positions into units and their size, directly impact daily learning. Other longer-term processes such as planning and control and decision-making authority, create an additional layer, where organizational memory is a critical asset.

In this section, we will address both the process of designing superstructures and their core components:

1. *The design process of superstructure units,* and key aspects when addressing this task to increase collective learning, in particular reflecting on a neglected lever: self-organization

2. *The grouping of units,* as a key lever to foster learning, including the Neural Paradigm principles supporting novel approaches to maximize the propagation of learning

3. *The sizing of the units,* where it is imperative to consider technology, which has been neglected as of today when it comes to organizational design, as a way to escape the limitations of our own human 'bounded rationality'

LEARNING SUPERSTRUCTURE DESIGN

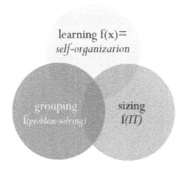

learning $f(x) =$
self-organization

grouping
(problem-solving)

sizing
$f(IT)$

DESIGN METHOD FOR LEARNING SUPERSTRUCTURES

'Let no one ignorant of geometry enter here' – PLATO[1]

Since Weber[2], designers have favored sequential approaches, when it comes to design methods. Like calculus, one first differentiates to understand the local patterns, and then integrates to grasp the accumulated behavior.

Superstructure design starts with differentiation, creating primary groups from individual positions, then addressing second-order units, often integrating those initial groups. The process iterates - as new organizational objects are created, the next layer integrates them. If there are inefficiencies, reordering and reintegration will follow.

The design process continues until the entire organization is encompassed, leaving a trail of formal authority systems and line reporting within the organization.

A traditional designer sees this activity as the formation of a bureaucratic skeleton, *a perfect order to stand the test of time.*

PERCEPTION:
LEARNING CAPABILITIES ARE PREDICTABLE

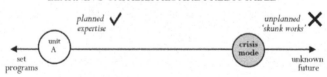

The Neural Paradigm: Self-Organization

As counterintuitive as it may be, the learning organization designer must consider an innovative and radically different approach when addressing knowledge-intensive realms.

Key principle: allow for self-organizing capabilities. This critical attribute embodies the essence of group learning, maximizing adaptability, communication fluidity and levels of autonomy not often found at scale in traditional organizations.

Self-organization is the ultimate configuration to facilitate group learning. It demands a level of autonomy largely absent in hierarchical set ups, with self-chartered pools of resourcing mobilizing across a number of key open-ended priorities.

REALITY:
MAJOR LEARNING CHALLENGES ARE UNPREDICTABLE

However, self-organization, while powerful and proven *(in areas such as research labs and consulting firms)* is notoriously difficult to prescribe. Why? Because it calls for the ability to delegate design into the organizational structure itself.

The alternative has been to turn a blind eye in the formal organizational chart and moonlight initiatives or create slack to be able to trigger 'skunk works' teams or its decisional sibling, the 'war room'. A suboptimal approach, nonetheless effective, that many organizations recur to when in crisis mode.

SR-71: 'SKUNK WORKS' AS AN ADAPTATION ISLAND

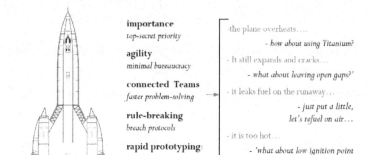

importance *top-secret priority*	the plane overheats....
	- *how about using Titanium?*
agility *minimal bureaucracy*	- It still expands and cracks...
	- *what about leaving open gaps?'*
connected Teams *faster problem-solving*	- it leaks fuel on the runaway...
	- *just put a little,*
rule-breaking *breach protocols*	*let's refuel on air...*
	- it is too hot...
rapid prototyping: *test concepts, iterate*	- *'what about low ignition point*
	fuel? We can use it as coolant!

match 3.3 *(maybe m 4⁺...)*

Military engineering organizations, like Lockheed Martin[3], have learned this the hard way — and after setting their 'skunk' expert tents outside manufacturing facilities, understood the need to formalize the process and give free reign to innovation.

In its extreme, a fully enabled learning organization needs to have a built-in ability to mutate. However, this concept is hard to harness, execute and endorse.

Who wants to invest in a moving target, that can be making cameras one day and then printers and copiers? *Or wait, are these the best companies ever?*

The superstructure of the learning organization has the ability to redesign itself, in parts or in whole. These capabilities operate at a higher level and shape new learning competencies:

1. The 'first plane' manifests visibly at the operational level, 'redesign' as a core corporate competency

2. The 'second plane' enables the first, by creates several instances of thematic, self-organizing talent pools.

THE 2nd PLANE: BENDING THE LEARNING CURVE

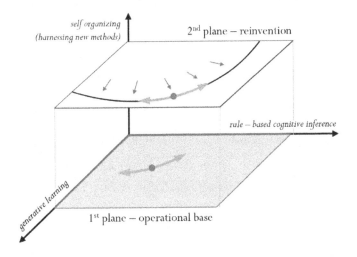

In mathematical terms, we can think about the second plane as enabling the second derivative of the learning rate – *it increases the acceleration of adaptation.* Major breakthroughs achieved are transported into the first layer, which will refine them further.

Just like a secret Blackbird prototype, getting towed from the 'Skunk Works' hangar in 1966, and going to production in 'Plant 4'. *Handing over a brilliant seed, that still needs a lot of operational learnings to flourish at scale.*

Leaders as Organizational Learning Designers

What is the role of leaders in this learning superstructures? Their mission is to hone the organization's capacities for self-design and self-organization, as a core competency. *Harnessing the talent, culture, and skills needed to function in this 'dual plane' mindset is incredibly challenging, yet immensely rewarding.*

Creativity, a commitment to learning and out-of-the-box thinking are some of the immediate traits that come to mind.

However, a critical, counterintuitive, learning leadership trait *is to perceive reality as it is* – not as the organization wants it to be. There is no self-organizing team, nor any learning design effort that will succeed if the 'espoused theory' *(the organization's perception of its capabilities and environment)* is different from the 'theory in practice'.

Designers operating in a dark organizational 'Johari's window' *(i.e., not knowing what they do not know about)* are doomed to fail. It is impossible to effectively engage the organization on a learning journey if the initiatives are not rooted in the reality of the strategic gaps and operational pain points. Such a journey invariably will backfire and raise learning barriers, fueled by skeptical staff not ready to embrace a change agenda they cannot relate to.

So, learning leaders are not just lofty, creative innovative types. *They need to live by the obligation to be realistic and do so in a way that does not betray the purpose of raising aspirational bars.*

GROUPING OF THE LEARNING UNITS

In the sequential method the first task is to differentiate the units. This task traditionally is based on executional work:

- ☐ Are the markets addressed compatible or adjacent?
- ☐ Are the processes interdependent with each other?
- ☐ Are there economies of scale by being together?
- ☐ Are the functions similar *(scope of work)?*

So, oversimplifying, traditional designers will almost unknowingly be checking the boxes that will fit the limitations of the 'bounded rationality' managers, operating manually.

And here is where 'corporate propaganda', rhetorical theories of intent, not anchored in reality compound to the design problem: Is Latam a region together with Canada, just to please the power vision of an 'Americas' executive? Or in reality, competitors understand Brazil is different in scale, language, and regulation, and would be better served together with other large emerging markets?

The oversimplification of legacy frameworks feels almost like a rushed 'multiple choice' exam. And the implications are dire, as these initial groupings have immediate implications on supervision, data flows, and confine many communications within base units, shaping the design of the remaining layers.

While these framework help to set basic operational units, they would fail to enable first-plane learning, much less creating self-organizing learning teams across the second plane.

Neural Network Paradigm: Grouping for Learning

In the Neural network Paradigm, a process would be evaluated by its complexity first addressed by multiple layers, able to process the complexity of the highly variable data vector being presented. We do a disservice by not matching skills or capacity with the complexity of the problems to be solved for.

Key learning considerations, such as the nature of the problem *(skill wise)* and the level of complexity of the problems *(depth)* need to be taken into account as primary drivers.

Under this approach, the grouping exercise for learning would look more as thoughtful diagnose and weighted scaled characterization of the spectrum of the problems to be solved:

- List key critical competencies to succeed in this function:
- Individuals: _____   _____   _____
  Processes: _____   _____   _____
  Systems: _____   _____   _____
- Estimate level of complexity required: _____
- Degree of competitiveness of function: _____
- Synergies with other *problem-solving* units across the org

_____ _____ _____ _____

...

☐ Are there clients & geos with similar problems?

_____ _____ _____

☐ Are there common methods to be shared?

_____ _____ _____

The whole emphasis of grouping should consider a 'Learning Strategy First' approach: The holistic inclusion of processes, systems and store knowledge is particularly relevant for complex problems that require team learning and go beyond the limitations of the individual rationality of teams and isolated experts in the first layer of groupings.

In the neural network model, a complex process is composed of multiple procedures generating a highly variable input vector. Structural modification through grouping can create specialized neuron teams with first-layer feedback.

Neural Network Paradigm Approach to 'Experts'

After the traditional design exercise, when unsolved dynamics are evident, often the solution would be to engage in expensive training or seeking to recruit the 'smartest person in the room'. This often results in multiple isolated individuals, optimizing local realms to their best capacity.

In rare occasions, those experts understand the need to team up and raise the collective thinking in the organization, and if successful getting empowered to go across lines, they may exert positive influence during a period of time.

Sadly, this reinforces the traditional paradigm: *Just address the symptom.*

The neural paradigm offers a powerful alternative, that may empower the system to solve unanticipated, complex problems, *at the expense of sacrificing some the generative capacity of the 'first plane' learning parasystems.*

Artificial neural scientists, should 'hack' this problem by creating and infusing specialized 'neurons' from the very first layer onwards and connecting them also to the less specialized cells across the network,

ATTENTIVE SPECIALISTS: ART RESONANCE EFFECTS4

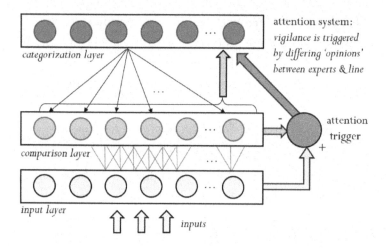

This approach is known as Adaptive Resonance Theory (ART) in Neural Networks. This connection scheme enables feeding the output of each specialized neuron in a layer back to all the neurons in that layer, *(or in a variant, to those at the same level that are spatially close),* while propagating it to others in the same class across other layers.

Learning by adaptive resonance is one of the fastest learning algorithms in Neural Networks. By retrofitting the outputs of neurons in the same layer to themselves, a faster convergence can be achieved.

Unfortunately, whenever we 'band aid' a learning system there is a price to pay:

- The stability of the network may suffer, different solutions optimizing for local minima will pop up
- Retrofitting them into a single optimized solution may be more expensive in the long run
- One misleading or lost feedback channel *(from experts in the first plane, in this case)*, can imbalance the system

In other words, there is not a proverbial 'free lunch' to replace the lack of proper design. *But in case of emergency, short-circuiting learning through expert 'war rooms', sharing data and empowering first-plane learning, can produce an effective 'stop the bleeding', and mitigate a learning crisis.*

SIZING UNITS TO INCREASE LEARNING

A critical aspect of traditional design is sizing the construct: How large should each unit be? And 'bounded rationality' kicks in again: *Human limitations condition how many individuals should report to a manager, and consequently influence the number of layers and sub-teams, given the breadth of work.*

Under the traditional paradigm, it's evident that increasing the size of units impacts learning:

- From the traditional perspective, learning occurs at the individual level, operating within a mesh of roles, and...
- Group learning happens when new knowledge is transferred from one organizational member to another

Under the conventional approach, unit growth is an enemy to learning, since communication becomes more formalized and standardized, reflecting limitations of human rationality.

The Middle Ages *'locked up'* wise people in monasteries, and their knowledge in siloed hand-written books. Guttenberg's print lowered the cost of shared knowledge, enabling a myriad 'intellectual flowers' bloom. *The Renaissance happened.*

How did we come to believe that 'small is better' to produce knowledge and adaptability? The more contributors, the better; the key is how to align sharing systems and incentives.

With modern technology, people are just an email away, they can contribute from anywhere in the world with lower costs than ever, yet reach outs in hierarchical orgs are often unwelcome, seen as futile or inappropriate. *Yet knowledge strives to continue to move forward*

The Neural Paradigm: Overcoming Size Restrictions

The key is to overcome historical rationality limitations: Can this limitation be overcome? We argue that it can.

Without dismissing the realities of historical human interactions and rooted 'aggregated' analytical behaviors, we believe it is possible to design larger units with highly fluid communication systems that channel contributions from a larger number of people, in a way that it would mutually offset individual's limitations.

The neural model thrives on propelling and sifting massive amounts of data, transparently to many actors: Our own brains, vastly outperform artificial neural network implementations: a human neuron can transmit its signal to 20,000 more neurons in the next layer, with switch times in the millisecond range.

Electronic and computational implementations are a million times faster but far less efficient computationally, needing multiple reprocessing to achieve pattern differentiation. A Very Large-Scale Integration (VSLI) transistor can propagate its output to just five or six other transistors, working at the limit of its power. Yet, learning algorithms overcome these limitations through software simulations of our neurons.

Similarly, designers must overcome communication paradigms confining the size of learning networks. Two main considerations:

1) the ability of each agent *(neuron equivalent)* to process a large number of input variables:

   - Do they have the training, space, and time to do so?

   - Is content collaboration an expected part of their roles?

2) the infrastructure to connect to many other elements of the network:
   - Information systems within the organization must be expanded to encourage sharing
   - Unfettered access is important, welcoming junior or more modest contributions, not just a few experts

Information Technology is poised to play a critical role. Computers are much more than number crunching devices to process payroll or perform complex mathematical modelling.

Modern relational databases, emails and posting boards are examples of mechanisms that can be embraced by organizations characterized by a lack of information sharing.

If learning-sharing of an entity is limited to their closest peers, this will shrink the network's learning capacity at both the systemic, parasystemic and metasystemic levels.

LEVERAGING INFORMATION TECHNOLOGY

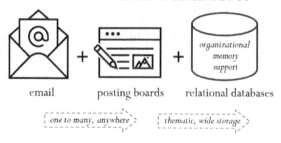

email   posting boards   relational databases

one to many, anywhere   *thematic, wide storage*

Information technology can reverse this situation, enabling information exchanges at an intensity that simulates small group intimacy but enriches it with many more participants.

- the output of any working unit, every report, log, or proposal can be made available in a relational database
- with just a few key words, information can be accessible to all, to understand the situation and suggest solutions
- team members can summarize digests and share broadly insights via posting boards and distribution lists these 'learning digests', backed up by sound data

So, even in a large global organization, at any level *(from operations to corporate)*, information can now be exchanged with an intensity typical of a small team in a 'skunk works' set up, benefitting from a much larger set of contributors.

SIZING UNITS TO INCREASE LEARNING

In summary, several propositions are formulated regarding the design parameters of the superstructure and learning:

1) The value of *a self-organizing capacity, including a 'second plane' layer*, able to reshape learning capabilities across the org
2) The importance of *grouping learning units reflecting problem solving needs rather than 'assumed' ones* to configure learning
3) The need *to leverage information technology when setting unit size, defying conventional trade-offs between size and learning*

Next, we shift focus from setting learning capabilities to operating them. *Picture a scenario, where an organization funded self-organizing pools of experts, built learning networks and sacrificed short-term 'Tayloristic' metrics, to enable front-line learnings...*

***

How do we set common plans & control execution? Can this learning construct operate cohesively, with multiple webs of communications popping up? The next stage addresses *how to align the learning ecosystem across these processes.*

11

PLANNING, CONTROL, AND COMMUNICATIONS
Empowering the Learning Ecosystem

P LANNING PROCESSES significantly influence the direction of the organization. They serve as the strategic compass, guiding the trajectory of growth and innovation.

Traditional design frameworks typically depict *planning processes as separate from control systems,* though they include some orchestrated touch points between them. After all, under this vision, *what is control other than tracking performance through a highly curated sequence of objectives, budgets, and process standardization, set by the 'perfect plan'...*

In the learning organization, we profess an entirely different approach. *Planning and control are not mere processes, but core competencies that must go hand in hand.*

In an adaptive organization, effective planning does not come solely from the hierarchy, nor does execution blindly follow the plan. It immediately informs any strategic reviews needed, as plans need to react to feedback.

Communications, or more properly, effective interrelations among units, are then the critical capability that holds smart planning and adaptive control together. It's through the steady flow of proper context, calibration, and emerging outcomes that teams can synchronize and rally around the goal.

Unfortunately, top-down hierarchical planning systems create passive cultures where aspirational goals, process improvements and learning systems stagnate. Also, associated formal communications have been prone to suppress inconvenient, external realities and 'out of the box' ideas.

This section discusses the *learning challenges posed by conventional planning, control and communication paradigms,* and how the Neural Paradigm can help us increase adaptability embracing a new paradigm around these core competencies.

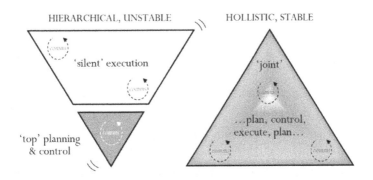

PLANNING AND CONTROL SYSTEMS

'Standards should not be forced down from above but rather set by the production workers themselves' – *TAIICHI OHNO*[1]

In many organizations, the traditional approach to planning & control follows a top-down methodology.

Here, the senior management delineates objectives which are then disseminated throughout the organization without meaningful feedback from the lower tiers. Control metrics are set accordingly, flowing all the way to the top, to be assessed in a quarterly or yearly cycle. Such a linear approach stifles the dynamism needed for continuous learning and adaptation.

Instead, a more inclusive method is recommended where a holistic vision for the organization emerges not just from the top-level view but amalgamating perspectives from all angles.

Such an approach enables bottom-up strategies that root their foundations in the diverse insights of employees at every organizational level.

This method prioritizes relevance, ensuring that plans and objectives closely align with the organization's real-world challenges and opportunities.

Additionally, by actively involving employees in decision-making, organizations can achieve a deeper sense of ownership and commitment, fostering an environment where every member feels their role is integral to the collective mission.

Structural Qualities of Planning in the Neural Paradigms

The Neural Paradigm for learning organizations relies on a metasystem acting as a central hub. Here's how it works:

1. *Aggregation of Featurized Content:* The various learning parasystems within the organization are constantly producing data based on their functions. Their output is *'featurized'*, depicting the essential patterns and characteristics of their specific insights.

2. *Processing and Synthesis:* The metasystem gathers this featurized content from all parasystems. Instead of just collecting metrics, the metasystem synthesizes content. This involves identifying patterns, correlations, and constraints provided by the different parasystems.

3. *Emergence of a Coherent Picture:* Through this continual synthesis of featurized content, the metasystem constructs a coherent and comprehensive picture of the organization's status, challenges, and opportunities.

4. *Guiding Planning and Controls:* With a comprehensive view in place, the metasystem produces rich content clusters to guide plans and controls more effectively. It ensures objectives are not just based on high-level views but informed by details coming from all levels.

In essence, the Neural Paradigm's strength lies in aggregating diverse, complex data streams, thereby enabling more adaptive planning and control mechanisms.

INTERRELATIONSHIP MECHANISMS

'Truth is found neither in the thesis nor the antithesis, but in an emergent synthesis which reconciles the two'— HEGEL[2]

Usually, when organizations identify a need for heightened coordination between units, they often respond by creating formal liaison roles or 'interconnection' mechanisms.

In traditional design, such structures, be they coordination roles, matrix configurations, or other formats, aim to bridge communication gaps.

Yet, these functions can inadvertently introduce challenges, leading to increased organizational complexity, creating siloed narratives to please top leaders, and being prone to power grabs and politics. Ultimately, they may stifle the spontaneous communications that often spark innovation.

In order to counter those dynamics, our best thinking today seeks to entice conducts rooted on shared values:

Fostering Team Learning and Dialogue: Team learning needs more than just cooperation; it demands genuine dialogue. Such dialogue is characterized by open communication, mutual respect, and a willingness to challenge and be challenged.

However, this is a long journey. Organizations take time to embrace a new culture. This spirit of dialogue needs to extend beyond individual teams, permeating inter-team interactions to really facilitate more adaptive control and decision-making.

Designing a learning organization isn't solely about crafting an optimal structural blueprint. It requires a nuanced understanding of what is *(and what is not)* being discussed:

- *The conversation topics:* Are those focused just on the 'functional responsibilities' risking an immediate sense of 'blame dynamics' *(e.g., it is about sales, not product)?*

- *Other dynamics at play:* Are leaders attuned to potential communication barriers, both structural and psychological? Is it *taboo* to point those barriers out?

Addressing these barriers involves setting communication channels around critical learning topics, where fact-based exchanges and collaborative problem-solving are the norm.

Learning Teams Interrelationships under the Neural Paradigm

The neural model's view on interrelationships can be viewed as a complex web of feedback loops, resembling a beehive:

PERVASIVE COMMUNICATIONS
across all learning parasystems…

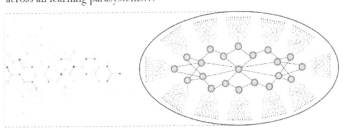

…WITH ENTIRE VISIBILITY
to the central metasystem

In the Neural Paradigm, there is a 'method to the madness'. Some of these loops are for learning, where planned outcomes and results may diverge, while others are more operational, relying on progress data. The metasystem monitors the 'hive', *seeking to prioritize learnings from both positive and negative outliers:*

1. *Feedback Web:* Each team, viewed as a node, both informs and receives feedback from other related teams, fostering a continuous cycle of learning and adaptation.

2. *Adaptive Responsiveness at the Metasystem Level:* With a focus on monitoring adaptive response, the metasystem ensures that all parasystemic teams are constantly interacting, integrating insights from each other.

3. *Pursuing Dynamic Equilibrium:* A balance is consistently sought. Disruptions within one team ripple across the network, prompting needed, fact-based, recalibrations.

Amidst this intricate network, *the emphasis remains on ensuring that the organization operates with coherence.* The metasystem's connections enable self-regulating mechanisms, keeping the system's equilibrium when facing challenges.

***

In essence, a dynamic, learning collective behaves like a 'swarm'. But in a successful, learning-oriented 'hive', who makes the decisions? That is our final subject: *Ensuring smarter decisions.*

12

DECIDING AND ACTING
MORE INTELLIGENTLY
Is it all about decentralization?

ANY ORGANIZATIONAL DESIGN METHOD must address the decision-making system. This activity is exponentially important when crafting learning organizations, thus making it an indispensable item in our toolkit. *The primary ambition behind our conceptualization of learning design is to enhance the quality, speed, and efficiency of collective decision-making.*

The conventional designer starts by scrutinizing the actors in play, *often with a decentralization bias*. After evaluating the level of autonomy each individual or team possesses and assessing the decision-making power topology within the organization, the typical focus is on addressing speed and curtailing repetitive cycles.

Organizational power is usually visualized located between two ends of a centralization spectrum:

TRADITIONAL UNIDIMENSIONAL PARADIGM
DECISION-MAKING: CENTRAL VS. DISTRIBUTED

a) At one end, we find *formal power*, characterized by a pronounced hierarchical influence over decisions:

   Top hierarchies make decisions, based on curated data fed to them, while front-line employees merely execute. In this setup, employees communicate the necessary information to their immediate superiors *(and evaluators)*. Eventually, the individual endowed with the requisite 'decision-making authority' (DMA) steps forward to act.

b) At the other end, lies *informal power*. This is frequently articulated by the autonomy granted to teams and individuals within the organizational fabric:

   In this mode, teams exchange more information horizontally, bypassing traditional reporting channels. They pool insights, engage in dialogue over options, and then decide and act, either collectively or autonomously.

Striking the right balance between these two aspects is considered critical when designing decision-making processes, and *typically captures the attention of traditional designers.*

The 'to be' paradigm shifted dramatically in recent times:

- The late XIX century, Tayloristic[1] views of the world heralded an era of *scientific management*, with optimally designed processes deployed centrally.

  This resulted in mass producing the Industrial Revolution's favorite governance model: Centralized, Weberian[2] bureaucracies, where most decisions are made by the upper echelons, with little input from the frontline

- Fast-forward to today's knowledge economy, where Drucker's[3] predicted *knowledge workers* reign supreme.

  the benefits of decentralization became clear, with the likes of Mintzberg[4] advocating for balance, to more extreme decentralization moves, as supported by Peter's and Waterman's *In Search of Excellence*[5] case studies.

  Even military analogies would support this thesis: From Napoleon's agile decision-making with field delegation, to today's highly appraised Israeli commandos, able to outthink centralized, traditional armies.

  From a learning perspective, it is tempting to just follow suit, loosely correlate decentralization with higher learning rates and declare success. After all, empowered experts deciding, and decentralized decision-making appears to result in more adaptive organizations.

Indeed, few learning barriers appear as potent *as decision-making processes inspired by mental models of an 'all seeing leadership' at the top:* Top hierarchies make decisions, based on curated data fed to them, while the front-line merely execute.

However, if teams close to the ground act independently without proper coordination, *the inefficiencies could be grueling. Neighboring* teams hacking problems may help each other, but proper knowledge takes time to travel through the system.

A sort of 'guerrilla warfare' model, *where highly effective cells may not be able to broadcast widely key insights, nor there may be incentives for other units to tap on them to accelerate learning.*

These decentralization shortcomings reveal the need to consider *two additional decision-making dimensions:*

- Memory: The capability to *share and leverage the richness of informal, distributed decisions, timely, across all teams*
- Accountability: A clear need for the vertical and horizontal teams to *participate in the learning feedback loop*

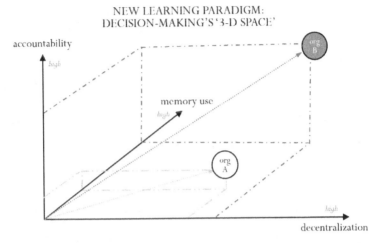

NEW LEARNING PARADIGM:
DECISION-MAKING'S '3-D SPACE'

Thus, designers should be also concerned about *the critical learning impact of shared accountability and collective memory.*

EMBRACING ADAPTIVE DECISIONS

The new learning paradigm upgrades decision making analyses *from a unidimensional space to a tri-dimensional one.*

In this new paradigm, it is not only about who or where the decisions are made, there is a mutual *interdependence between learning and decision-making processes.*

- Are decision-makers relying on learned criteria, reflecting previously captured and stored knowledge? Do they log cases that may require departing from tradition, to experiment?
- Are they incented when creating learning assets *(regardless of success of failure),* and also for scaling up quickly successful new patterns?

Adaptive decisions (either centralized or decentralized), need to be recognized as a process of trial and error, where decision-making and learning processes interact through two mechanisms:

1. Organizational memory *(expressed as systems, policies, and formalized procedures that support ex-ante decision-making),* and

2. Feedback loops allowing decision-makers to evaluate the results of their decisions, learn from them, and be accountable.

An increased learning rate is possible by acting on these two additional levers *(learning efficiency and intensity will benefit from reusability and aligned incentives).* Why is so difficult then? Why vicious downward cycles, losing core competencies, are ao prevalent? There may be a correlation between concentration and the ability to unfold the other two dimensions.

TRADITIONAL VIEW: ME, ME, ME...

It is all about the Centralization of Power

Within most organizations, managers are exposed to incentives that promote consolidation of power. Rationally, they aim to increase coordination and control, resulting in a *winner-takes-it-all* dynamic, where decision-making discretion remains concentrated around a few individuals.

At the extreme, decisions are made by a 'brain' at the top, and the rest of the organization merely implements them. This creates a massive decision-making bottleneck:

Decisions are delayed: Information takes time to ripple through the system, more so vertically (*time).*

Information is filtered: Upward reporting *(to your own evaluators)* may not help exemption and attribution of causality *(quality).*

Decision-making faces bandwidth issues: Top managers, constrained by *bound rationality,* can only focus on key decisions, leaving many issues unaddressed (*cost).*

And this configures the ultimate delusion: Under the false impression of a great Pareto optimization *(where a few decide on a handful of the most important decisions)*, a long queue of tightly interrelated issues rests unattended.

This 'learning trap' stifles adaptability and innovation, as often new trends go undetected, until it is too late to address them.

THE DECISIONAL 'PARETO MIRAGE'

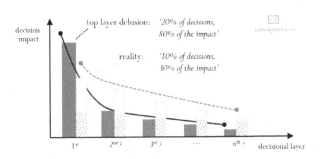

'Do not be afraid to make a decision,
do be afraid not to make a decision' - AKIO MORITA

Morita-san could not have phrased it better. Great danger lies in the decisions 'not made'. The illusion of Pareto efficiency deludes top managers into believing effective governance is in place. As the graph depicts:

- rarely do the majority of the problems reach to the top,
- *a good fraction of them have interdependencies that would require joint decisioning across multiple levels*
- *even the fraction that gets lined up to be decided at the top,* risk exceeding the capacity of top executives

Unfortunately, adding to the complexity, a beleaguered top decentralizes decisions too late, without a complete purview.

Prey to a delusional trap, traditional designers will add a bit more power for middle layers *(vertical decentralization)*, reshape some roles to declutter flows *(horizontal decentralization),* and a *pyrrhic victory will be declared: A smaller decision queue at the top.*

EFFECTIVE DECENTRALIZATION FOR LEARNING

'Better a witty fool, than a foolish wit' - *SHAKESPEARE*[7]

Regrettably, for the designer of the learning organization, the root issue remains unresolved: The overload on senior executives is not the problem; it's a symptom of a serious structural flaw.

These organizations display a complete lack of understanding of learning as a system, the interdependencies of decisions and the need to incentive teams to work across the organization and leverage shared experiences, to achieve better decisions.

The traditional mental model of individual, top deciders betrays, alone, the purpose of collective learning: The world is divided between a few *'capable' (decision-makers)* and *'incapable' (implementers)*. Compounding the issue, top decision-makers are often insulated from the consequences of their poor decisions since they control both the structure and the narrative, *leading to valuable learnings from the ground-level being overlooked.*

This situation resembles a Quixotic saga[9] *or a Shakespearean comedy of errors,* with missteps from the top perpetuated by design...

top layer delusion:

- *'there are at least 30 outrageous giants...'*

- *'the giants metamorphosed in windmills, to deprive me of the honor of the victory'*

bottom layer realism:

- *'what giants? There are not giants but windmills'*

- *'I feel the pain of your worships' disaster as much as if it had been my own...'*

Decentralization will not be effective unless it addresses the underlying issues that inhibit the functioning of the adaptive decision-making cycle. Fortunately, it is possible to strengthen it by supporting learning enablement systems in two ways:

1. *Shared Accountability Across Vertical Feedback Loops:* Setting feedback loops when delegating formal decision-making power is pivotal. *This approach ensures the entire vertical line learns from and co-owns both successes and failures. It fosters shared ownership of outcomes and stimulates experimentation.*

   As each member, team, and unit in the organization, regardless of level, jointly benefits from the correct decisions and shares the consequences of wrong ones, the rate of systemic learning increases. *We regard this as a constructive iteration of the 'Groupthink' syndrome, which underpins sustainable and positive collective learning.*

2. *Enablement of Informal Power and Nurturing Organizational Memory:* Empowering horizontal units can amplify the assimilation rate of new information. However, it's paramount that systems and processes record ongoing activities to facilitate knowledge sharing.

   Organizational Memory, at the horizontal plane, emerges as a pivotal facilitator. Stored knowledge, whether in technology, processes, or policies, refines decision-making. Only with this foundation, horizontal decentralization can become an effective accelerator, and maintain learning integrity; ensuring all the distributed process is captured, from the initial data processed to distributed outcomes.

   Synergistic Decision Decentralization Under the Neural Learning Paradigm he Neural Paradigm

In the neural learning paradigm discussed, *executive functions are not just distributed but intrinsically interconnected.*

Operational and strategic decisions are conducted by agile, distributed parasystems, which operate under the oversight of the learning metasystem. This dynamic balance ensures that operational decisions benefit from proximity to action, making them timely and accurate, while being recalibrated.

When it comes to strategic decisions — those that make us rethink our objectives — the breadth of decentralization guarantees a comprehensive approach in constraint assessment.

THE COLLECTIVE LEARNING SYSTEM AS A BRAIN

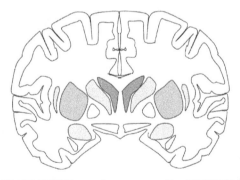

LEARNING PARASYSTEMS structured
similarly to primary sensor cortex areas ...

(akin to a multilayer neural network -> feature)

... connected by a METASYSTEM, like the
corpus callosum, communicating all units

(akin to a Hoppfield network -> patterns)

A recurring motif in the learning organization, affecting also decision-making, has been the tension between expanding decentralization, while maintaining cohesive communications. This issue touches the very essence of growth dynamics, which often result in complexity increases and decayed performance.

***

The antidote lies in carefully crafted information systems. Central to our proposition of Collective Learning are smart systems that not only bridge communication gaps but also *foster synergistic connectivity through a vast network of content contributors.*

Conclusion

COLLECTIVE LEARNING: A NEVER-ENDING JOURNEY?

C APTURING THE ESSENCE OF THE FRAMEWORK discussed is no small feat. Traditional organizational learning, focused on individual training, is becoming less effective. Recent approaches offer somewhat minor updates but miss the intrinsic nature of collective adaptation. Many of the case studies that fascinate strategists today frequently defy full explanation, partly ignoring the new learning structures methods appearing in front of us.

Meanwhile, emerging computational models rooted in cybernetics offer unprecedented promise to map and engage in 'learning by design'. These advances indicate a future where designing, tracking and improving structures to optimize information processing and foster collective organizational learning will be not only possible but also critically important.

Similarly to designing a production system today, *it will be critical in the future to map out what information needs to be captured, how it needs to be interpreted, and how to store* and continuously evaluate the organization's learning capability.

Innovations in computational learning, especially neural network models, present exciting new opportunities. These systems' data-centric approaches release collective learnings from the boundaries of human limitations and conflicts of interest. Their dynamic plasticity and self-learning capabilities deepen our understanding of how collectives can best capture fact-based performance information and consider critical adaptation features necessary for increased competitiveness.

Yet, implementation is a significant challenge. It demands strategic support from the highest levels of the organization. This strategic support is necessary for the transition to a collective learning paradigm, a journey that promises to be highly iterative, coming with its own learning opportunities.

The method we propose in this work is just an idea, a thesis, *that needs further development and real-world testing.* The ideal toolkits, communications and incentives between the learning design teams, the core functions they are seeking to improve, and top leadership, should be rigorously evaluated.

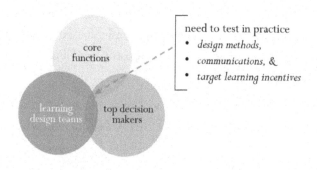

need to test in practice
- *design methods,*
- *communications, &*
- *target learning incentives*

We need a structured understanding of where to create, how to integrate, and strengthen the interaction between key learning capabilities in order to establish the optimal structural parameters for enhancing the learning process. That in itself is a daunting journey for the organizational learning designer and their counterparts alike.

For insight into this formidable task, we turn to an unexpected source, also from Japan – not a celebrity CEO or a top consultant this time, but an enduring master from ancient times: Miyamoto Musashi, the undefeated Samurai. In 1632, he wrote in *'The Book of Five Rings[1]:'*

> *'The world is in a constant state of change. Nothing in the world 'is' a certain way, but rather 'is transforming' into it. The nature of reality is a process, a continually changing flow...*
>
> *However, the reality of things is not always evident: Behind the apparent void lies the totality of possibilities. Only through the way of Heihō, the path of virtuosity, consisting of continuous commitment to truth, self-affirmation, and the practice of a boundless vision, can you understand your role in the process.*
>
> *By keeping an open mind, you'll rhythmically accompany the flow in tune with the compass of change. The goal is to continue on the endless path of ongoing perfection, where you'll be able to master any technique without the need for a master.'*

Musashi's words offer valuable insights for designers aiming to strengthen organizational learning: the importance of observing the non-obvious, continuously practicing reaffirmation, and maintaining an open mind while reevaluating the process.

The 'rings' *(scrolls)* capturing his quest for life-long success, called to excel in five areas: *Earth, Fire, Water, Wind and Void:*

の巻 - THE FIVE SCROLLS

地 *earth* foundational martial principles

火 *fire* tactics, conflict dynamics

水 *water* form and adaptability

空 *void* thoughtless self awareness

風 *wind* critique and self assessment

Master Miyamoto Musashi

Borrowing Master Musashi's wisdom, organizations cannot be just Earth and Fire *(i.e., basic processes and execution)*. Those are important, *'the basics'* if you will, *but to set up an extraordinary journey, we need Water, Wind, and Void.* These three learning rings complement the execution-oriented ones, and are the key components of a successful, continuous learning journey.

Musashi's teachings seem to offer considerable applicability for designers focused in strengthening organizational learning: *the ability to capture the workings of the system, observing the non-*

obvious, revise your forms and the continuous practice of reaffirmation.

There is no right or wrong if you keep adapting and innovating your learning processes, empowering teams to leverage novel technologies and find ways to help individuals to self-organize, formalize their learning connections and knowledge assets, and view themselves as a learning unit.

Failure seems to be guaranteed by stillness and stiff hierarchies, operating with hindered data fueling the illusion of perfection. These learning monopolies can perpetuate outdated rule-based systems, effectively holding back the evolution to cooperative, collective learning organizations.

ORGANIZATIONAL LEARNING'S DESIGNER SCROLLS

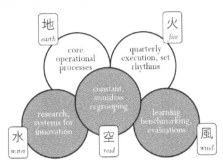

Therefore, all these disciplines, both old and new ones, intentionally revised, designed and integrated, would contribute to find our way of *Organizational Learning Heihō*:

> *The Path of Continuous Improvement of organizational learning processes, where the goal is not to reach any specific end state but to remain on the endless path of harmonious transition between increased awareness states*

***

This, we believe, should be the true calling of committed Organizational Learning Designers, seeking to succeed by *defying existing constraints and advancing in their own transformation journeys.*

Epilogue

2023 REFLECTIONS
Why does a 30-year time capsule matter?

DECEMBER 7TH, 2023. Today, I finished translating and *(aesthetically)* updating my old thesis. *I must confess that I have rewritten this section many times during the eight weeks that the whole process took,* from scanning the original 1993 thesis manuscript in Spanish, to e-publishing the English version.

After all, this is one of the very few sections in this book, *together with the preface and the introduction,* in which I can use my somewhat improved '2023 voice' with complete freedom; not worried about adding content not present in my original working papers, adding a case study not discussed in the MBA, or struggling not to reword any phrases in a way that would distort its original meaning.

In the spirit of self-assessment, prior versions of this Epilogue included 'right & wrong prediction' tables, lists of 'applicable & not-so-applicable' frameworks, or even 'recommended chapters or frameworks' for 2023 readers.

Perhaps Simon would smile at the futile attempt of my *very bounded rationality,* trying to write an unbiased epilogue. *Who am I to disagree with the tenants of such a distinguished a Nobel prize?*

Yet, re-reading Cicero's advice, dated 46 BC, seemed to solve all the early difficulties with this section.

> *'To be ignorant of what occurred before you were born is to remain always a child. For what is the worth of human life, unless it is woven into the life of our ancestors by the records of history? — CICERO[1]*

Every memory is useful — *right or wrong* — and, as this work advocates for, these experiences are the very foundation of successful learning, individual and collective. So, this section has evolved more appropriately into a 'thank you' section:

- I am most grateful that some of these past thoughts have been documented, and that some have found part of these helpful.

- Personally, I feel blessed for the chance to rejoin my younger self, almost a 'Disney's The Kid'[2] experience. A forgotten box may bring your *'twenty-something-year-old-self'* to life.

- And I also feel incredible gratitude for all the opportunities that I have to be an actor in today's world of AI. The field staged an unbelievable 'comeback' enabled by:

  - Inexorable Moore's law dynamics, lowering compute power. *VLSI yesterday, Cloud today, Quantum tomorrow*

- Fastly evolving topologies and attention frameworks, *CNNs yesterday, GPTs today, Energy Networks tomorrow*
- Enabled by unlimited, frictionless access to knowledge *RDBMs yesterday, Vector DBs today, Quantum DBs tomorrow*

We truly stand today at the epicenter of a new, colossal Renaissance.

A revolution marked by an seemingly uncontrollable acceleration of new discoveries, with their complexity exceeding our bounded rationality, where the collective fabric of learning that Collaborative humans and AI *(ChAI)* agents weave will hold the understanding of the whole. And the challenge remaining, for all the mere parts of that equation, is to create a collective that will serve the common good.

Now more than ever, the imperative to increase the learning rate is out there, and some world-class players have started systematically tracking individual and team predictive power.

And the unprecedented power of Generative AI technologies, unveiled at scale earlier this year, posts a very profound dilemma:

In a world were collective, machine-enabled learning surpasses the learning capability of the majority of the individuals *(even within their bounded rationality limits):*

- *How do we rethink and evolve our own capability to learn?*

- *What are the limits we can pursue within our own biology?*

- *Is augmentation, cybernetic or genetic, our inescapable future?*

- *Will most of us become polymaths, focused on integrating AI-driven technologies we cannot apprehend? Or,*

- *Will 'deep specialists' thrive, adding a temporary edge that AI cannot bridge, and learn to evolve quickly or become obsolete?*

- *How will economies evolve to incorporate the shifting value added of population segments?*

- *Will all of this matter when The Discontinuity happens?*

• To stay abreast of many of these dynamics, we recommend following the shapers and makers of our current AI fabric:

- Zuckerberg, Thiel, Pichai, Andrew Ng, Musk, Fei-Fei Li, Delangue, Bezos, Altman and Amodei have excellent informed perspectives to offer.

- Following key researchers such as Vaswani, LeCun, Goodfellow, Hinton, and Anandkumar, among several others, is a good way to gain some foresight.

• Also, AI regulation is coming into play, with the US, the EU *(published just yesterday)* and China issuing executive orders, directives and guidelines respectively.

- These developments are welcome, since they allow an opportunity window to ensure safe AI development.

- We have tamed dangerous technologies in the past through regulations and controls; *however, often after learning firsthand of their dangers through a disruptive event.*

- From electricity to nuclear power, *examples abound of exaggerated fears, unknown perils, and singularities that triggered change.*

For the time being, one thing is for sure:

> *This new wave is not only about incorporating rapidly evolving technology but embracing deep change across human and artificial collective learning through these groundbreaking paradigm.*

From today's 'mobile first' institutions taking over well-established incumbents in traditional industries, to metaverse plays or blockchain constructs, *the emergence of a 'deep digital twins' world, where the virtual counterpart is richer and more sophisticated than the real one is becoming a reality.*

Our own personal virtualization is reshaping our ability to compete successfully in the future.

As of now, it appears connected to our ability to shape our professional and personal profiles to fit into this increasingly competitive environment.

As for what we can do today, we must wake up to the fact that all the investments done in 'Big Data' and AI to date, were just the preamble of a much more ambitious *'AI First'* journey.

a new ecosystem: llamas, vicunas and alpacas grazing around pinecones

For all the advice about 'bi-focal' approaches (i.e. launching short-term initiatives, while preparing longer-term ones), this is our take:

- Large Language Models (LLMs) need to be incorporated aggressively and piloted *(natively, as a service or both)*
- It is imperative to rearchitect internally the organization to create and retain knowledge *(a broader exercise than just calling an external service, while preserving privacy).*

People, Processes and Systems need to be redesigned holistically.

Which takes us to our current line of research *(unsurprisingly perhaps): The Design of Learning Organizations,* in the era of Generative AI.

1. As systems understand language, the interaction between machine learning and human is becoming seamless

2. Interactive training can happen both ways – AI being trained by humans and *vice versa*, no longer the monopoly of the *'Data Scientist'* but the realm of *'Data Citizens'*

3. No-code frameworks will deepen the *automation of communication and analytical flows in the organization*

As a result, a plethora of hybrid parasystems and metasystems is emerging *(now really practical hybrid, Collaborative Human-Artificial Intelligence 'ChAI' constructs)*, live operational cases and real assessed impact.

Customer experiences will be reshaped, hyper-personalization front and center, so contextually-rich, yet frictionless interaction will characterize the flows of organizations able to ride this wave of change.

And their figures of value potential and strategic impact promise more than Kaizen, Kanban and all the Six Sigma methodologies combined.

Current estimates from the McKinsey Global Institute[3] herald ranges between 12% to 15% of global revenue across knowledge-intensive industries.

That potentially would hint a larger change over the next five years than what the Internet and mobile have generated over the last twenty.

Plenty of reasons to get excited and mobilized around building the Intelligent Organizations capable of harnessing this change in the near future.

***

Thank you once again for your attention and we will love to hear your thoughts about this work and ideas for the future. This era also enables collaborative interaction between authors and readers. *We welcome your comments, questions and ideas at:*

- <u>LinkedIn: Alex_Picos</u>
- <u>Intellixens.com - The Institute for Safe ChAI</u>
- *<u>TheDesignofLearningOrganizations@gmail.com</u>*
- Or, just use the barcode below to land on our laboratory page – eager to learn about your thoughts, proposal and ideas, to 'brew' great and safe ChAI

Acknowledgments

Brigida and Alexander Picos, my beloved wife and son who provide me with daily support, ideas, inspiration and patience as I worked on this book and its draft sequel simultaneously.

Maria Luisa and Gaspar Picos, my dear parents, who made the highest sacrifices to support me in a (then most uncommon) career path.

Chetan Nadgire for encouraging me this year to publish a book, while discussing novel AI architectures and all the PayPal family echoing that thought.

Belkis Lopez, Mercedes Angarita, David Schwartz and Giorgio Trettenero, who supported relaunching this work with the FIBA and FELABAN audiences.

Juan Antonio Bustillo and Lorenzo Lara for being great advisors and endorsing a crazy topic 30yrs back: organizations modelled on, and around AI.

Ricardo Hausmann, Roberto Rigobon, Edgar Osuna, Ramon Pinango, Alan McAdams and Ana Maria Leizaola for elevating my journey at IESA and Cornell.

Fernando Bello, Oscar Baez, Juan Alcazar and Beatriz Meneses Palenzona, for encouraging me to speak my mind, and write this thesis, always offering advice to make the work relevant and tangible.

Luis Da Silva, Emilio Otermin, Marco Cutin, (and their parents and families) for being amazing though partners on any topic, back then, and over time.

Lazaro Recht and Robert Moo King, for teaching me at college how to think with rigor, mathematically and ethically, and to the USB family at large.

Elena Quesada, German Vásquez and all my IBM ELT class for supporting my trip to the 1991 Neural Network Congress in Paris and many other learning opportunities, including making my MBA journey possible.

Vera Gavizon, and all the McKinsey family, for supporting my journey at Cornell and launch my career post MBA, and to Vanina Bruno, who I met there in 1994, and reappeared as a 'Godsend' 30 years later to upgrade our visuals!

And to the great leaders fueling the journey that followed these thoughts!

Truly yours, onwards, always

Glossary

Preface: 1993 AI-Driven Thoughts

AI (ARTIFICIAL INTELLIGENCE): The simulation of human intelligence processes by machines, especially computer systems.

COLLECTIVE LEARNING PARADIGMS: Approaches where groups or communities learn together, sharing and accumulating knowledge.

CORNELL: Cornell University, an Ivy League university located in Ithaca, New York.

FINTECH: A blend of "finance" and "technology" that refers to any business that uses technology to enhance or automate financial services and processes.

GENERATIVE TECHNOLOGIES: Technologies that use algorithms to generate new content or data that resemble defined datasets.

IESA: Instituto de Estudios Superiores de Administración, the top business school and managerial think tank in Caracas, Venezuela.

IT (INFORMATION TECHNOLOGY): The use of systems (especially computers and telecommunications) for storing, retrieving, and sending information.

MAINFRAMES: Powerful computers used primarily by large organizations for critical applications, typically bulk data processing such as census, industry and consumer statistics, enterprise resource planning, and financial transaction processing.

MCKINSEY & CO.: A global management consulting firm that serves a wide range of private, public, and social sector institutions.

MCKINSEY DIGITAL: The digital and analytics arm of McKinsey & Company, providing services in digital transformation and helping organizations harness technology for growth and innovation.

MBA (MASTER OF BUSINESS ADMINISTRATION): A graduate degree focusing on business administration and investment management.

NEURAL NETWORKS: A series of algorithms that attempt to recognize underlying relationships in a set of data through a process that mimics the way the human brain operates.

OIL AND GAS RESERVOIR SIMULATIONS: Computational methods used to estimate reserves and predict the flow of fluids (typically oil, water, and gas) through porous rock formations underground.

PALO ALTO: A city in California known for its tech industry presence, home to Stanford University and in the heart of Silicon Valley.

PAYPAL: An American company operating a worldwide online payments system that supports online money transfers. (Stock ticker: PYPL).

SMART CREATIVES: A term often used to describe individuals who combine technical knowledge with creativity and are adept at working in the fast-paced and dynamic environment of technology companies.

STANFORD: Stanford University, a private research university in Stanford, California.

Introduction to the original work

ADAPTIVE LEARNING: An approach where learning methods and experiences are tailored to the learner's needs and can evolve based on their progress.

ARGYRIS, CHRIS: An influential academic known for his groundbreaking work in organizational learning and human behavior. He served as a professor at Harvard Business School when he introduced the concept of Double Loop Learning in his work 'Theory in Practice' (1974) with Donald Schön.

ARTIFICIAL NEURAL NETWORKS: Computational models inspired by the human brain, used in machine learning and artificial intelligence. These networks simulate the way biological neural networks in the human brain process information.

BRAIN SCIENCE: The study of the brain's structure, function, and development, often in the context of understanding learning and cognition.

COLLECTIVE LEARNING: Learning that takes place at the organizational or group level, as described in this work. It integrates individual learning experiences to create new organizational knowledge.

COMPETITIVE ADVANTAGE: A business concept referring to the factors that allow an organization to produce goods or services better or more cheaply than its rivals.

INFORMATION PROCESSING: Refers to the process of gathering, manipulating, storing, retrieving, and classifying recorded information.

INSTITUTIONAL MEMORY: The collective knowledge and learning of an organization, including its history, experiences, and operational practices.

INTELLIGENT COMPANIES: Businesses that utilize data, analytics, AI, and other smart technologies to inform decision-making and strategy.

ORGANIZATIONAL LEARNING: As defined in this book, it's the process by which organizations acquire the capability to respond to new or evolving known situations, evaluate and improve on their collective learning, while leveraging a shared memory to store, retrieve and refine knowledge.

SENGE, PETER: A bestselling author and senior lecturer at MIT's (Massachusetts Institute of Technology) Sloan School of Management. Senge is acclaimed for his work *The Fifth Discipline* (1990), where he introduced Systems Thinking and Mental Models, among other concepts.

XIX CENTURY 'INDUSTRIAL REVOLUTION': Refers to the period of major industrialization that took place during the 19th century, significantly impacting business and society.

CHAPTER 1: Organizational Learning

ADAPTATION ROUTINES: As noted in this book, these are procedures through which organizations adapt their core operations based on collective experiences and learning.

BOUNDED RATIONALITY: A concept developed by Herbert A. Simon, professor at Carnegie Mellon University. This theory suggests that human decision-making is constrained by limited information, time, and cognitive abilities. Simon was awarded the Nobel Prize in Economic Sciences in 1978.

CHAIN OF COMMAND: The hierarchical structure within an organization, which is essential for understanding decision-making processes and knowledge sharing.

CHALLENGER DISASTER: A tragic event in the realm of space exploration that occurred in 1986. The catastrophe was largely attributed to organizational failures, specifically the loss of critical maintenance routines and the overlooking of increasing risk factors associated with failing components.

CODIFICATION: As discussed in this work, the process of systematically capturing and documenting knowledge within an organization.

COMMUNICATION NETWORK: As used in this book, the pathways through which information and knowledge are shared within an organization.

DOUBLE LOOP LEARNING: Introduced by Chris Argyris and Donald Schön in 1978. Argyris was a professor at Harvard Business School, and Schön was a researcher at MIT. The concept involves not just solving problems but questioning the underlying assumptions that cause them.

DRUCKER, PETER (1909-2005):: A seminal thinker, influential writer, and management consultant. Drucker held a professorial role at Claremont Graduate University and is renowned for his work 'The Practice of Management' (1954).

GAME-CHANGER: An element that significantly alters an existing situation. This term is frequently used in strategy to describe disruptive innovations.

GESTALT: A psychological term highlighted in this work to describe how collective action can surpass individual contributions, meaning the whole is greater than the sum of its parts.

GROUPTHINK: Concept introduced by Irving Janis in 1972, who was a professor at Yale University. Groupthink is a psychological phenomenon where the desire for group cohesion leads to poor decision-making.

HEBBIAN LEARNING: A foundational idea in neural network theory, neurobiology, and psychology, encapsulating how learning can occur without explicit guidance. If two neurons activate together frequently, the strength of the synaptic connection between them increases.

INDUSTRY TURMOIL: A state of high disturbance within an economic sector, requiring swift and adaptive organizational learning.

INDIVIDUAL LEARNING: Personal acquisition of knowledge or skills through study and experience. It is an important contributor to the organizational learning process but is not synonymous with it.

JANIS, IRVING: A psychologist and professor at Yale University, best known for introducing the concept of Groupthink in 1972.

MASLOW, ABRAHAM: A groundbreaking psychologist best known for introducing Maslow's Hierarchy of Needs. He held a faculty position at Brandeis University when he developed his seminal work.

MENTAL MODELS: A concept introduced by Peter Senge, a senior lecturer at MIT (Massachusetts Institute of Technology) Sloan School of Management. Mental models are deeply ingrained assumptions or generalizations that affect our understanding and actions.

MILLIKEN, FRANCES J.: A professor at New York University's Stern School of Business, co-author of *Challenger: Fine-tuning the odds until something breaks*. The paper highlights the dire risks of losing organizational memory.

STARBUCK, WILLIAM H.: Co-author of the Challenger paper with Milliken. He was also affiliated with New York University's Stern School of Business at the time of the paper's publication.

NEURAL LEARNING: As covered in this work, this concept from brain studies and computer science refers to the adaptive learning process of neural networks. It serves as a metaphor for how organizations can adapt and learn.

ORGANIZATIONAL LEARNING RATE: A metric introduced in this work to quantify the speed at which an organization adapts to new information or challenges.

ORGANIZATIONAL LEARNING SYSTEM: As mentioned in this work, it is an integrated set of processes and structures that facilitate collective learning. It's measurable in terms of efficiency, speed of adaptation, and quality of outcomes.

ORGANIZATIONAL MEMORY: As defined in this work, this refers to the collective stored information within an organization, whether in human minds, documents or systems, accessible to improve future decision-making.

PARADIGM: As outlined in this book, a set of assumptions, concepts, values, and practices that constitute a way of viewing reality.

REFLECTION-IN-ACTION & REFLECTION-ON-ACTION: Concepts introduced by Donald Schön, a researcher at MIT. They involve real-time reflection during an activity (reflection-in-action) and post-activity reflection to consider improvements (reflection-on-action).

SATISFICE: A term closely associated with bounded rationality, introduced by Herbert A. Simon, a professor at Carnegie Mellon University. It's a decision-making strategy that aims for a satisfactory or good-enough result rather than the optimal one.

SCHÖN, DONALD: An influential researcher at MIT, Donald Schön co-developed the concept of Double Loop Learning with Chris Argyris and introduced Reflection-in-Action and Reflection-on-Action.

SHIFTING THE BURDEN PATTERN: A concept introduced by Peter Senge, which focuses on understanding how individual parts of a system interrelate and work within the context of larger systems.

SIMON, HERBERT A.: A Nobel laureate in Economic Sciences (1978), Herbert A. Simon was a professor at Carnegie Mellon University. He is best known for his work on bounded rationality.

SOFT FACTOR: As noted in this book, these are intangible elements like culture and social interaction that contribute to organizational learning but are hard to measure directly.

STRATEGIC OUTCOMES: As mentioned in this work, these are the long-term goals that an organization aims to achieve. Effective organizational learning positively influences these outcomes.

SYSTEMS THINKING: A concept developed by Senge, Systems Thinking aims to understand how individual parts of a system interrelate and function within the broader system, essential for modelling performance improvement.

CHAPTER 2: Competitiveness and Learning

1973 GAS PRICE HIKES: Refers to the oil crisis of 1973, where a drastic increase in oil prices had a significant impact on the global economy. The chapter suggests that automakers who adapted their product lines to more fuel-efficient models after the crisis saw increased market share.

AMERICAN MANAGEMENT ASSOCIATION (AMA): A not-for-profit, membership-based management development organization based in the United States. AMA offers a variety of training programs, seminars, and resources designed to improve individual and organizational performance.

ATTRITION: The natural reduction of the workforce due to factors like resignations and retirements. In this context, it's important because higher attrition rates can lead to a 'Learning Death' spiral by disrupting the flow of institutional knowledge.

BONAPARTE, NAPOLEON: A French military leader and Emperor known for his role in the Napoleonic Wars and the expansion of the French Empire. The chapter cites two quotes from different phases of his life. The first quote, 'From the sublime to the ridiculous is but a step,' was from his rising years during the Italian Campaign, a set of early military operations that underpinned the rise of the French Empire. The second quote comes from his time on Elba, an island where he was exiled and effectively a prisoner, illustrating the fragility of success and leadership.

CANON: A multinational corporation headquartered in Tokyo, Japan, specializing in optical, imaging, and industrial products such as cameras, copiers, and printers (Stock ticker: CAJ). The company is known for its focus on continuous learning and the development of new core competencies, which have made it a leader in several markets.

COMPETITIVE RIVALRY: A component of Michael E. Porter's Five Forces model, which refers to the competition between existing firms in an industry. High competitive rivalry can make an industry less attractive in terms of profitability.

CORE COMPETENCIES: These are unique capabilities that confer competitive advantages to an organization. These competencies often arise from an organization's collective skills and learning and are critical for long-term growth and sustainability.

COST OF OWNERSHIP: This term describes the total cost incurred by owning a product or service, including its purchase price, maintenance, and operating costs. This concept is crucial in consumer decision-making processes and also for organizational procurement strategies.

CYCLE OF SURRENDER: Coined by Hamel and Prahalad, it describes a pattern where companies facing threats generate delayed or partial responses, eventually leading to a degenerative process impacting competitiveness.

DARWIN, CHARLES: A 19th-century British naturalist renowned for his contributions to evolutionary biology. Darwin's groundbreaking work, 'On the Origin of Species,' introduced the concept of natural selection as the mechanism for evolution.

DARWINIAN FATALISM: A term used to describe the idea that organizations must adapt and learn or face decline and possible extinction. It is analogous to the 'survival of the fittest' concept in evolutionary biology.

DETROIT: A city in Michigan, USA, formerly a world-class hub for automotive innovation, often cited as a cautionary tale for failure to adapt and innovate.

FIVE FORCES: A model developed by Michael E. Porter that identifies five forces that influence an industry's competition: supplier power, buyer power, competitive rivalry, threat of substitution, and the threat of new entry.

GENERAL MOTORS CORPORATION (GM): An American multinational automotive corporation (headquartered in Detroit, Michigan; stock ticker: GM). The chapter cites GM as an example of an industrial giant suffering from low learning rates and poor functional connectivity, which led to its decline.

GO-TO-MARKET STRATEGIES: Plans and actions that dictate how a product is sold and distributed to customers. The text suggests that superior go-to-market strategies, informed by learning, can provide a significant competitive edge.

HAMEL, GARY: A prominent business thinker known for his pioneering work on innovation and corporate strategy. He introduced the concept of 'strategic intent' in his article titled 'Strategic Intent' with co-author C.K. Prahalad. Hamel was affiliated with the London Business School around the time the article was published in 1989.

HARVARD BUSINESS REVIEW (HBR): A leading journal based in Boston, Massachusetts, known for its high-impact articles on business management and strategy. The journal is affiliated with Harvard University and has been a gold standard for thought leadership in corporate strategy.

HONDA: A multinational corporation headquartered in Tokyo, Japan, primarily known for its automobiles and motorcycles (Stock ticker: HMC). Honda is noted for its focus on learning and innovation, especially in technologies like VTEC (Variable Valve Timing & Lift Electronic Control) for improved engine performance and efficiency.

JOHNSON SCHOOL LIBRARY, CORNELL UNIVERSITY: Located in Ithaca, New York, this library is notable for its extensive collection of business and management literature. It is affiliated with Cornell's MBA program, and the library is now named XYZ.

KOMATSU: A multinational corporation headquartered in Tokyo, Japan, specializing in construction, mining, and military equipment (Stock ticker: KMTUY). Komatsu is known for its focus on organizational learning to develop new core competencies, allowing it to compete effectively on a global scale.

LEXISNEXIS: A legal and public-records database used for academic and journalistic purposes. It also offers critical resources for business research and is available at many university libraries.

MILAN: A city in Italy known for its luxury fashion industry, including the production of luxury handbags. It serves as an example of an environment where core processes and functions are shaped by the availability of talent.

ORGANIZATIONAL AMNESIA: As defined in this work, a loss of institutional knowledge, often due to high attrition rates or lack of mechanisms to preserve and transfer knowledge.

PORTER, MICHAEL: A leading scholar in economics and management, known for theories on economics, business strategy, and social causes. He has served as a professor at Harvard Business School and has received numerous awards, including the McKinsey Award for the best Harvard Business Review article.

PRAHALAD, C.K.: A distinguished business scholar particularly known for his work on corporate strategy and the role of top management in shaping it. He frequently collaborated with Gary Hamel and co-authored the article 'Strategic Intent,' which is seminal in the study of organizational learning. Prahalad was affiliated with the University of Michigan's Ross School of Business at the time the article was published.

RESEARCH & DEVELOPMENT (R&D): The directed efforts within a business to innovate, introduce, and improve its products and processes. R&D is often cited as a key area for organizational learning, as it enables firms to develop new core competencies.

SILICON VALLEY: A region in California, USA, known for its high-tech industry, including software, hardware, and internet companies. It serves as an example of an innovation hub where competitive products and services are developed.

SMALL AND MEDIUM BUSINESSES (SMBS): Companies with a smaller number of employees and lower revenue compared to large corporations. They are often nimbler and can adapt faster due to their size.

SONY: A multinational conglomerate corporation headquartered in Tokyo, Japan, known for its consumer electronics (Stock ticker: SNE). The corporation has been highlighted for its commitment to innovation and learning, particularly in rapidly evolving markets.

STRATEGIC INTENT: A concept introduced in an article by Gary Hamel and C.K. Prahalad, which refers to a long-term vision that energizes and motivates an organization to achieve a competitive edge.

SURVIVAL OF THE FITTEST: A phrase originating from Charles Darwin's theory of natural selection. It is used in business to describe the cut-throat competition among firms where only the strongest survive and thrive.

CHAPTER 3: Learning 'By Design'

ADAPTIVE CONTROL: A type of control in systems theory that adjusts in response to changes in the external environment and the system itself.

CYBERNETIC THEORY: A theoretical framework dealing with the structure, constraints, and possibilities of regulatory systems. Often used in the context of adaptive control of multi-variable nonlinear systems.

FEEDBACK LOOP: A mechanism in the design process that allows for periodic evaluation and adjustment of the learning models and strategies in use.

IMPLEMENTATION MODEL: The final phase in the design process of learning organizations, focusing on operationalizing the learning strategies and integrating them into the daily operations of the organization.

LEARNING BY DESIGN: A structured approach to enhancing organizational learning, involving the integration of learning capabilities within an organization's structure and processes.

MULTI-VARIABLE SYSTEMS: Systems that involve multiple inputs and outputs, requiring complex coordination and analysis to understand and control.

NONLINEAR SYSTEMS: Systems in which the output is not directly proportional to the input, often characterized by complex interactions and feedback loops.

PRESCRIPTIVE MODEL: A phase in designing learning organizations that involves crafting tailored solutions to specific learning challenges, based on insights from cybernetic theories and other advanced methodologies.

REPRESENTATIONAL MODEL: In the context of organizational learning, a model that provides a detailed analysis of an organization's current learning processes and challenges, often using principles from artificial intelligence and microeconomics.

SYSTEMIC THINKING: A method of understanding and analyzing complex systems by considering the interactions and relationships between system components, rather than focusing on individual parts in isolation.

CHAPTER 4: Modeling Learning Organizations

DYNAMIC SYSTEMS: A mathematical and computational approach to understanding complex systems characterized by changing, often nonlinear interactions among their components.

GENERATIVE LEARNING: A type of learning where new knowledge or solutions are created, often through innovative thinking or problem-solving approaches.

INFORMATION REVOLUTION: A period marked by rapid advancements in information technology, significantly impacting communication, data storage, and processing capabilities.

JAY FORRESTER: A pioneering American engineer and systems scientist, recognized for his foundational work in the field of system dynamics.

LEARNING ORGANIZATION MODELS: Conceptual frameworks or representations that illustrate the processes and structures supporting learning within organizations.

METASYSTEMIC LEARNING: A higher-level learning process within an organization, where the learning mechanisms oversee and adjust the activities of organizational subsystems or parasystems. It involves autonomous goal-setting and parameter generation based on situational assessments.

PARASYSTEMIC LEARNING: Distributed learning systems running parallel to an organization's core operating units, facilitating continuous learning and adaptation.

QUAESTOR: In ancient Roman times, an official responsible for various administrative and financial duties, often symbolizing a paradigm of moral authority and rational decision-making.

REACTIVE LEARNING: Learning that occurs in response to specific situations or problems, often characterized by adaptation to existing knowledge or practices.

SCHÖN'S TECHNICAL RATIONALITY: A concept by Donald Schön referring to a decision-making process based on logical analysis and empirical data, often used in contrast to more intuitive or experiential approaches.

SYSTEM THEORY: An interdisciplinary study of systems in general, with the goal of elucidating principles that can be applied to all types of systems at all nesting levels in all fields of research.

SYSTEMS MODELING: The process of creating abstract models of complex systems, often using mathematical and computational techniques, to study their behavior and interactions.

TAYLORISTIC ORGANIZATIONS: Organizations structured and managed based on the principles of scientific management as proposed by Frederick W. Taylor, focusing on efficiency and productivity through task specialization.

CHAPTER 5: Parasystems: The Foundation

CHALLENGE DEMAND SPACE: A conceptual framework for analyzing the types and frequencies of challenges an organization faces, used to determine the learning needs.

EDGEWORTH BOX: A tool adapted from economics, used here to represent the optimal allocation of learning resources over time in an organization.

LEARNING - DESIGNABILITY FRONTIER: Also the 'L&D' frontier, a conceptual boundary that represents the efficient mix of learning paradigms, balancing costs and benefits.

LEARNING ISOQUANTS: Lines in a conceptual learning space representing equal levels of learning capacity, irrespective of the mix of learning types.

LEARNING PARASYSTEM: A parallel system within an organization that supports core processes by processing information and facilitating learning.

MARGINAL LEARNING UTILITY: The additional benefit gained from an investment in learning, critical for assessing the value and impact of learning initiatives.

MEMORISTIC FACTORS: Components that enhance an organization's memory and formalized processes, including training, standardization, and rule-based systems.

OPTIMAL LEARNING POINT: The point at which an organization's learning capacity and challenges intersect, indicating the most effective learning mix.

PARETO EFFICIENCY IN LEARNING: A state where resources are allocated in such a way that it's impossible to improve anyone's learning without reducing someone else's.

QUEVEDO, FRANCISCO DE (1580–1645): A Spanish writer and poet, known for his wit and baroque style, quoted here for his insights into the power and influence.

PROBLEM COMPLEXITY: The degree of difficulty and variability inherent in challenges faced by an organization, influencing the type of learning required.

RULE-BASED COGNITIVE INFERENCE: A learning type that relies on applying established rules and knowledge to solve problems, particularly effective for routine issues.

CHAPTER 6: Metasystem: The Orchestrator

CREATIVE TENSION: A concept in organizational learning that describes the gap between an organization's current reality and its aspirations or goals.

DARWINIAN ENVIRONMENT: A term used to describe highly competitive and rapidly changing business environments, akin to Darwin's theory of natural selection.

ENERGY DYNAMICS IN LEARNING: The application of energy principles to understand and analyze learning processes in organizations.

FAKE EQUILIBRIUMS: Refers to misleading or unstable states of balance within organizational learning systems.

LEARNING - DESIGNABILITY FRONTIER (L&D): A conceptual model used to determine the most efficient mix of learning paradigms in an organization, balancing costs and benefits.

LEARNING METASYSTEM: An overarching system within an organization that coordinates and integrates learning across various subsystems.

MARGINAL RATE OF SUBSTITUTION: An economic concept used here to describe the balance between different types of learning activities in an organization.

PARETO, VILFREDO: An Italian economist known for the Pareto principle or 80/20 rule, which is applied here to understand learning optimization in organizations.

POTENTIAL ENERGY IN LEARNING: A metaphorical concept used to describe the buildup of capacity or tension in an organization's learning system, leading to significant changes.

RESISTANCE IN LEARNING: The concept of organizational barriers and challenges that hinder or slow down the learning process.

TESLA, NIKOLA (1856–1943): A Serbian-American inventor, electrical engineer, and futurist, known for his contributions to the design of the modern alternating current (AC) electrical supply system, quoted for his views on energy and innovation.

VON HELMHOLTZ, HERMANN (1821–1894): A German physicist and physician, renowned for his conservation of energy principle, which is applied here in the context of learning systems.

CHAPTER 7: Underlying Structures

PATTERN RECOGNITION: The ability to detect and interpret patterns in data. In organizational learning, it plays a crucial role in understanding complex scenarios and contributing to decision-making processes.

HOLLERITH, HERMAN: Known for his significant contributions to early computing and data processing. Hollerith was an American inventor who developed an electromechanical punched card tabulator to assist in summarizing information and, later, accounting. He was a key figure in the development of the modern automatic computation.

SCHIAPARELLI, GIOVANNI: An Italian astronomer noted for his study of Mars. He was known for his detailed observations of the Martian surface, including his controversial identification of 'canali' on Mars, which fueled speculation about Martian life.

STRUCTURES OF METASYSTEMIC LEARNING: Refers to the organizational structures and mechanisms that facilitate complex and nuanced learning paradigms at the metasystem level. These structures guide and adjust the learning processes of organizational subsystems.

STRUCTURES OF PARASYSTEMIC LEARNING: The organizational framework supporting learning at the parasystem level. Characterized by adaptability, these structures are built upon layers of information processing units that contribute to the collective learning process.

CHAPTER 8: Neural Networks

ALCMAEON OF CROTON (Born c. 510 BC, death date unknown): An early Greek medical theorist and philosopher, often regarded as the founder of anatomy. He was one of the first to assert that the brain, not the heart, was the center of intelligence.

ARISTOTLE (384–322 BC): An ancient Greek philosopher and scientist, one of the greatest intellectual figures of Western history. He believed the heart was the center of human intelligence, not the brain.

DONALD HEBB (1904–1985): A Canadian psychologist who contributed significantly to the field of neuropsychology and is best known for his theory on how neurons in the brain strengthen or weaken their connections.

FRANK ROSENBLATT (1928–1971): An American psychologist known for developing the perceptron, an early type of artificial neural network, in 1957.

GALILEO GALILEI (1564–1642): An Italian astronomer, physicist, and engineer, sometimes described as a polymath. Galileo played a major role in the scientific revolution during the Renaissance.

GIOVANNI BATTISTA VENTURI (1746–1822): An Italian physicist, economist, and diplomat known for the discovery of the Venturi effect in fluid dynamics.

HERMANN VON HELMHOLTZ (1821–1894): A German physicist and physician, renowned for his wide-ranging contributions to science, especially the conservation of energy, and the theory of electrodynamics.

METASYSTEMS: In the context of organizational learning, metasystems refer to overarching systems that integrate and manage multiple subsystems within an organization.

NIKOLA TESLA (1856–1943): A Serbian-American inventor, electrical engineer, mechanical engineer, and futurist best known for his contributions to the design of the modern alternating current (AC) electricity supply system.

PARASYSTEMS: In organizational theory, parasystems are subsystems or components within an organization that work alongside main systems to support and enhance their function.

PLATO (424 – 348 BC): An ancient Greek philosopher, student of Socrates, and teacher of Aristotle, who founded the Academy in Athens, the first institution of higher learning in the Western world.

SANTIAGO RAMÓN Y CAJAL (1852–1934): A Spanish neuroscientist and pathologist, awarded the Nobel Prize in Physiology or Medicine in 1906 for his work on the structure of the nervous system.

CHAPTER 9: Instrumenting Foundational Design

ADAPTIVE FORMALIZATION: A concept in organizational design that refers to systems capable of preserving organizational memory and learning without limiting necessary flexibility.

HOPFIELD NETWORKS: A type of recurrent artificial neural network popularized by John Hopfield in 1982, known for its pattern recognition abilities.

JOHN HOPFIELD: An American scientist known for his invention of the Hopfield Network, a form of recurrent artificial neural network.

JUST-IN-TIME KNOWLEDGE: A training approach focusing on providing information and skills to organizational members exactly when they are needed.

LEARNING JOB SPECIALIZATION: A concept in organizational design focusing on the specialization of job roles to enhance learning and adaptability.

MANHATTAN PROJECT: A research and development undertaking during World War II that produced the first nuclear weapons. Often cited in organizational studies for its innovative, multidisciplinary approach.

NELSON AND WINTER (1982): Richard R. Nelson and Sidney G. Winter, authors known for their work on evolutionary economics. They proposed viewing organizations as repertoires of skills.

PERCEPTRON MODEL: An early type of artificial neural network developed by Frank Rosenblatt, consisting of a single layer of artificial neurons.

PETER SENGE: An American systems scientist known for his work on learning organizations, particularly through his book "The Fifth Discipline."

POSITION DESIGN: The process of defining the roles, responsibilities, and requirements of specific job positions within an organization.

SYSTEMIC THINKING: A cognitive approach that involves understanding and managing complex systems by recognizing interdependencies and interactions.

TRAINING AND INDOCTRINATION: Processes within organizations aimed at developing skills, knowledge, and aligning members with organizational values and culture.

CHAPTER 10: Designing the Learning Superstructure

ADAPTIVE RESONANCE THEORY (ART): A learning algorithm in Neural Networks characterized by retrofitting the outputs of neurons in the same layer to themselves, facilitating faster convergence.

GROUP LEARNING: The process where new knowledge is transferred from one organizational member to another, often in a collaborative setting.

JOHARI WINDOW: A tool used to understand interpersonal communication and relationships, particularly within organizations.

NEURAL PARADIGM: A framework that uses principles from neural networks and brain function to understand and design organizational structures and learning systems.

SELF-ORGANIZATION: The process where a structure or pattern appears in a system without a central authority or external element imposing it, often as a result of internal dynamics or interactions among system components.

SKUNK WORKS: A term originally used by Lockheed Martin to describe their advanced development programs, now widely used to describe a group within an organization given a high degree of autonomy to work on advanced or secret projects.

SR-71 BLACKBIRD: A long-range, high-altitude, Mach 3+ strategic reconnaissance aircraft developed by Lockheed Martin's Skunk Works.

WAR ROOM: In organizational context, a physical or virtual space where strategic decisions are made, often used in crisis management or complex project planning

CHAPTER 11: Planning, Control, and Communications

ADAPTIVE RESPONSIVENESS: A characteristic of learning organizations where systems adjust and respond to changing environments and internal feedback.

FEEDBACK WEB: In the Neural Paradigm, a network of continuous feedback loops among teams for learning and adaptation.

GEORG WILHELM FRIEDRICH HEGEL (1770-1831): A German philosopher who made significant contributions to philosophy, particularly in the development of dialectics.

INTERRELATIONSHIP MECHANISMS: Structures and processes in an organization that facilitate communication and coordination between different units.

LEARNING COLLECTIVE: A group or organization that actively engages in shared learning and adaptation.

METASYSTEM: In the Neural Paradigm, a central hub that aggregates, processes, and synthesizes data from various parts of an organization to guide planning and controls.

PLANNING AND CONTROL SYSTEMS: Organizational processes that guide the direction, monitor performance, and adjust strategies as needed.

TAIICHI OHNO (1912-1990): A Japanese industrial engineer and businessman known as the father of the Toyota Production System, which became Lean Manufacturing in the West.

TEAM LEARNING AND DIALOGUE: A process where members of a group collectively enhance their capabilities and understanding through open communication and mutual respect.

CHAPTER 12: Deciding and Acting More Intelligently

ADAPTIVE DECISION-MAKING: A process where decisions are made considering the changing environment and feedback, emphasizing flexibility and responsiveness.

CENTRALIZATION OF POWER: The concentration of decision-making authority at the upper levels of an organization's hierarchy.

COLLECTIVE MEMORY: The shared pool of knowledge and information held by the members of a group, which grows over time and contributes to the group's understanding and decision-making processes.

DECENTRALIZATION: Distribution of decision-making authority throughout an organization, often to lower-level managers or teams.

FORMAL POWER: The official power given to individuals within an organization based on their position or role.

INFORMAL POWER: The influence and authority an individual may have that is not officially sanctioned but arises from relationships within the organization.

MINTZBERG, HENRY (BORN 1939): A Canadian academic and author on business and management, known for his work on organizational structure and strategy.

MORITA, AKIO (1921-1999): A Japanese businessman and co-founder of Sony Corporation.

OHNO, TAIICHI (1912-1990): A Japanese industrial engineer and businessman, considered to be the father of the Toyota Production System, which inspired Lean Manufacturing in the Western world.

PARETO OPTIMIZATION: A concept in economics and engineering referring to the allocation of resources to optimize multiple objectives without making one aspect worse off to improve another.

SHAKESPEARE, WILLIAM (1564-1616): An English playwright, poet, and actor, widely regarded as the greatest writer in the English language and the world's greatest dramatist.

TAYLORISTIC VIEWS: Refers to the principles of scientific management developed by Frederick W. Taylor, emphasizing efficiency, standardization, and a top-down approach to management and labor.

WATERMAN, ROBERT: A business theorist known for his work on organizational development and effectiveness, particularly in the context of corporate culture.

Conclusion: A Never-Ending Journey?

HEIHŌ *(the path of virtuosity):* A concept from Musashi's teachings, emphasizing continuous commitment to truth, self-affirmation, and the practice of a boundless vision to understand one's role in the process of change.

MUSASHI'S FIVE RINGS: A metaphorical concept from Miyamoto Musashi's teachings, representing different aspects of mastery and learning: *Earth, Fire, Water, Wind, and Void.*

MUSASHI, MIYAMOTO: Renowned Japanese swordsman and philosopher, Miyamoto Musashi (c. 1584 – 1645) authored 'The Book of Five Rings,' a seminal text on martial arts and strategy. Musashi is celebrated for his mastery in duels and his deep commitment to Bushido, the way of the warrior.

Epilogue: 2023 Reflections

ALTMAN, SAM: CEO of OpenAI, a leading artificial intelligence research lab. Known for his contributions to advancing AI technology and promoting safe AI development.

AMODEI, DARIO: Co-founder of Anthropic, an AI safety and research company. Known for his work in AI safety and ethics, particularly in developing reliable, interpretable, and steerable AI systems.

ANANDKUMAR, ANIMA: Director of Machine Learning Research at NVIDIA and a professor at Caltech. Recognized for her work in tensor algorithms and probabilistic models in AI.

BEZOS, JEFF: Founder of Amazon and a key figure in technology and e-commerce. His insights into AI stem from Amazon's extensive use of AI in its operations and services.

BIG DATA: Refers to extremely large data sets that may be analyzed computationally to reveal patterns, trends, and associations, especially relating to human behavior and interactions.

CHAI (Collaborative Human-Artificial Intelligence): A concept referring to the synergistic collaboration between humans and AI systems, enhancing decision-making and problem-solving capabilities.

DELANGUE, CLÉMENT: Co-founder and CEO of Hugging Face, a leading company in the field of natural language processing (NLP) and AI. Known for democratizing access to state-of-the-art NLP tools and models.

FEI-FEI LI: Co-Director of Stanford University's Human-Centered AI Institute. Known for her work in computer vision and AI ethics, particularly for her role in developing ImageNet.

GOODFELLOW, IAN: Known for inventing Generative Adversarial Networks (GANs). His work significantly contributes to the field of deep learning and generative models in AI.

HINTON, GEOFFREY: A professor emeritus at the University of Toronto and a researcher at Google Brain. One of the pioneers of deep learning, especially known for his work on neural networks.

LARGE LANGUAGE MODELS (LLMS): Advanced AI models capable of understanding and generating human-like text, used in various applications like translation, content creation, and conversation agents.

LECUN, YANN: CHIEF AI Scientist at Facebook (Meta Platforms, Inc.) and a professor at New York University. A prominent figure in AI, especially known for his work on convolutional neural networks.

MUSK, ELON: CEO of Tesla and SpaceX, known for his ambitious projects involving AI, such as autonomous vehicles and space exploration technologies.

NG, ANDREW: Co-founder of Google Brain, former Chief Scientist at Baidu, and founder of Coursera. A leading figure in AI, particularly known for his work in deep learning and education in AI.

PICHAI, SUNDAR: CEO of Alphabet Inc. and its subsidiary Google, overseeing the company's advancements and applications in AI technologies.

QUANTUM COMPUTING: A revolutionary computing technology that uses the principles of quantum mechanics. It holds potential for solving complex problems much faster than classical computers.

RDBMS (Relational Database Management System): A database management system based on the relational model, widely used for storing and managing structured data.

THIEL, PETER: Co-founder of PayPal and an influential figure in the tech industry. Known for his investments and insights into AI and its impact on society and the economy.

VASWANI, ASHISH: Known for his co-authorship of the influential paper "Attention Is All You Need," which introduced the Transformer model, a key development in natural language processing.

ZUCKERBERG, MARK: Co-founder and CEO of Facebook (Meta Platforms, Inc.), leading the company's initiatives in AI, particularly in areas like content moderation and virtual reality.

Notes

Introduction to the original work

1. Argyris, Chris, *Overcoming Organizational Defenses*, (Boston, Massachusetts: Allyn & Bacon, 1990

2. Peter Senge, *The Fifth Discipline: The Art and Practice of the Learning Organization*, New York: Doubleday, 1990)

CHAPTER 1: Organizational Learning

1. Espasa-Calpe. *Diccionario enciclopédico universal ilustrado*. Madrid, 1979

2. Janis, Irving L. *Victims of groupthink: A psychological study of foreign-policy decisions and fiascos*. Houghton Mifflin Harcourt, 1972

3. Beckhard, Richard, and Reuben T. Harris. *Organizational Transitions: Managing Complex Change*. Boston: Addison-Wesley, 1987

4. Milliken, Frances J., and William H. Starbuck. *The Contingency Theory of Organizations*. Academy of Management Review 2, no. 2, 1977

5. Simon, H., Bounded Rationality and Organizational Learning, Organization Science, Volume 2, No. 1, February 1991

6. Argyris, Chris, and Donald A. Schön. *Organizational Learning: A Theory of Action Perspective*. Reading, MA: Addison-Wesley, 1978.

7. Senge, Peter, *The Fifth Discipline: The Art and Practice of the Learning Organization,* (New York, New York: Doubleday, 1990

CHAPTER 2: Competitiveness and Learning

1. Michael E. Porter, *The Five Competitive Forces That Shape Strategy*, HBR 1979

2. Gary Hamel & C.K. Prahalad, *Strategic Intent*, HBR, 1989

3. Robert S. Kaplan & David P. Norton, *The Balanced Scorecard, Measures That Drive Performance,* Harvard Business Review, 1992

4. Masaaki Imai, *Kaizen: The Key to Japan's Competitive Success,* Harvard Business Review, 1986

5. Jon R. Katzenbach & Douglas K. Smith, *The Discipline of Teams,* Harvard Business Review, 1993

6. David A. Aaker, *Managing Brand Equity,* Harvard Business Review, 1991

7. Hirotaka Takeuchi & Ikujiro Nonaka, *The New New Product Development Game,* Harvard Business Review, 1986

8. George Stalk, Philip Evans & Lawrence E. Shulman, *Competing on Capabilities: The New Rules of Corporate Strategy,* HBR, 1992

9. Chris Argyris, *Teaching Smart People How to Learn,* HBR, 1991

10. Theodore Levitt, *The Globalization of Markets,* HBR, 1983

11. Deming, W. Edwards. *Out of the Crisis.* Cambridge, MA: MIT Press, 1986

12. Chandler, David G. *The Campaigns of Napoleon.* Scribner, 1966

13. American Management Association. 1992. *Survey on American Competitiveness.* Chicago: American Management Association

CHAPTER 3: Learning 'By Design'

1. Forrester, Jay W. Industrial Dynamics. Cambridge, MA: MIT Press, 1961.

2. Ramon y Cajal, Santiago. *Histologie du Système Nerveux de l'Homme et des Vertébrés.* Paris: A. Malone, 1909-1911

CHAPTER 4: Modeling Learning Organizations

1. Forrester, Jay W. *Industrial Dynamics.* Cambridge, MA: MIT Press, 1961.

2. *Records of the Office of Strategic Services,* Washington DC, National Archives, 1947

3. Aristotle. *De Anima.* Translated by R. D. Hicks. Cambridge: Cambridge University Press, 1907

4. Crawford, Michael. The Roman Republic. 2nd ed. Cambridge, MA: Harvard University Press, 1992

5. Taylor, Frederick Winslow. *The Principles of Scientific Management.* New York: Harper & Brothers, 1911

6. Doyle, Arthur Conan. A Scandal in Bohemia. In The Adventures of Sherlock Holmes, 15-36. London: George Newnes Ltd., 1892

7. Schön, Donald A. *The Reflective Practitioner: How Professionals Think in Action.* New York: Basic Books, 1983

8. Imai, Masaaki. Kaizen: The Key to Japan's Competitive Success. New York: McGraw-Hill, 1986

9. McAteer, P., *Simulations: Learning Tools for the 1990s,* Training & Development, Volume 45, October 1991

10. Cicero, Marcus Tullius. *De Oratore.* Translated by E.W. Sutton and H. Rackham. Cambridge, MA: Harvard University Press, 1942

CHAPTER 5: Parasystems: The Foundation

1. Michael E. Porter, The Five Competitive Forces That Shape Strategy, (Harvard Business Review, 1979

2. Senge, Peter M. "The Fifth Discipline: The Art & Practice of The Learning Organization." Currency Doubleday, 1990

3. Ramon y Cajal, Santiago. Histologie du Système Nerveux de l'Homme et des Vertébrés. Paris: A. Malone, 1909-1911

4. Kroc, Ray. *Grinding It Out: The Making of McDonald's.* St. Martin's Paperbacks, 1987

5. Friedman, Milton, and Rose Friedman. *Free to Choose: A Personal Statement.* New York: Harcourt Brace Jovanovich, 1980

6. Marshall, Alfred. *Principles of Economics.* 8th ed. London: Macmillan and Co., Ltd., 1920

7. Doyle, Arthur Conan. *The Adventure of the Copper Beeches.* In The Adventures of Sherlock Holmes, 272-313. London: George Newnes Ltd., 1892

8. Pareto, Vilfredo. *Manuale di Economia Politica con una Introduzione alla Scienza Sociale. Milano:* Società Editrice Libraria, 1906

9. Edgeworth, Francis Ysidro. *Mathematical Psychics: An Essay on the Application of Mathematics to the Moral Sciences.* C. Kegan Paul & Co., 1881

10. Chandler, David G. The Campaigns of Napoleon. NY: Macmillan, 1966

11. Quevedo, Francisco de. "Obras completas de Francisco de Quevedo." Editorial Aguilar, 1981

CHAPTER 6: Metasystem: The Orchestrator

1. *The Dutch Disease.* The Economist, November 26, 1977

2. von Helmholtz, Hermann. *On the Sensations of Tone as a Physiological Basis for the Theory of Music.* Longmans, Green, and Co., 1885 (English translation).

3. Tesla, Nikola. *My Inventions: The Autobiography of Tesla.* Hart Brothers, 1982

4. Hutchins, E., 'Organizing Work by Adaptation', (Organization Science, Volume 2, No. 1, February, 1991

CHAPTER 7: Underlying Structures

1. Schiaparelli, Giovanni. "Life on Mars." Translated by Richard McKim. London: Faber and Faber, 1982

2. Hollerith, Herman. "An Electric Tabulating System." In "The Quarterly Journal of the Library of Congress," edited by Daniel Hammer. Washington, D.C.: Library of Congress, 1976

3. Beer, Stafford. "Brain of the Firm: The Managerial Cybernetics of Organization." London: The Penguin Press, 1972

CHAPTER 8: Neural Networks

1. Galen. On the Functions of the Parts of the Human Body. Translated by Margaret Tallmadge May. Ithaca, NY: Cornell University Press, 1968

2. *The Complete Works of Aristotle:* The Revised Oxford Translation, edited by Jonathan Barnes, Vol. 1. Princeton, NJ: Princeton University Press, 1984

3. Gall, Franz Joseph. *On the Functions of the Brain and of Each of Its Parts.* Translated by Winslow Lewis Jr. Boston: Marsh, Capen & Lyon, 1835

4. Sömmerring, Samuel Thomas von. *Über das Organ der Seele.* Königsberg: Friedrich Nicolovius, 1791

5. Golgi, Camillo. *Sulla struttura della sostanza grigia del cervello.* Gazzetta Medica Italiana Lombardia, 33, no. 244 (1873): 244-246

6. Ramón y Cajal: *Historia de una voluntad.* TV mini-series. Spain, 1982

7. McCulloch, Warren S., and Pitts, Walter. *A Logical Calculus of the Ideas Immanent in Nervous Activity.* Bulletin of Mathematical Biophysics 5, 1943

8. Hebb, Donald O. *The Organization of Behavior: A Neuropsychological Theory.* New York: Wiley & Sons, 1949

9. McCarthy, John; Minsky, Marvin; Rochester, Nathaniel; Shannon, Claude. *A Proposal for the Dartmouth Summer Research Project on Artificial Intelligence.* 1955

10. Rosenblatt, Frank. *The Perceptron: A Probabilistic Model for Information Storage and Organization in the Brain.* Psychological Review 65, no. 6, 1958

11. Ivakhnenko, A. G., and V. G. Lapa. *Cybernetic Predicting Devices.* Washington DC, US Department of Commerce, 1965

12. Minsky, Marvin, and Seymour Papert. Perceptrons: *An Introduction to Computational Geometry*. Cambridge, MA: The MIT Press, 1969

13. Fukushima, Kunihiko. *Neocognitron: A Self-organizing Neural Network Model for a Mechanism of Pattern Recognition Unaffected by Shift in Position*. Biological Cybernetics 36, no. 4, 1980

14. Kohonen, Teuvo. *Self-Organized Formation of Topologically Correct Feature Maps*. Biological Cybernetics 43, no. 1. 1982

15. Rumelhart, David E., Geoffrey E. Hinton, and Ronald J. Williams. *Learning Representations by Back-Propagating Errors*. Nature 323, 1986

16. LeCun, Yann, et al. *Handwritten Digit Recognition with a Back-Propagation Network*. In *Advances in Neural Information Processing* Systems 2, San Mateo, CA: Morgan Kaufmann, 1990.

17. Hopfield, John J. *Neural Networks and Physical Systems with Emergent Collective Computational Abilities*. *Proceedings of the National Academy of Sciences* 79, no. 8, 1982

18. Cohen, Michael A., and Stephen Grossberg. *Absolute Stability of Global Pattern Formation and Parallel Memory Storage by Competitive Neural Networks*. IEEE Transactions on Systems, Man, and Cybernetics, no. 5, 1983

CHAPTER 9: Instrumenting Foundational Design

1. Rhodes, Richard. *The Making of the Atomic Bomb*. New York: Simon & Schuster, 1986

2. Nelson, Richard R., and Sidney G. Winter. *An Evolutionary Theory of Economic Change*. Cambridge, MA: Belknap Press of Harvard University Press, 1982

3. Shannon, Claude E. *A Mathematical Theory of Communication*. Bell System Technical Journal 27, 1948

4. Schlegelmilch, Rainer, and Hartmut Lehbrink. *Grand Prix: Fascination Formula 1*. Cologne: Könemann, 1993

CHAPTER 10: Designing the Learning Superstructure

1. Plato. *The Republic*. Translated by G. M. A. Grube. Indianapolis: Hackett Publishing Company, 1992

2. Weber, Max. *Economy and Society: An Outline of Interpretive Sociology.*. Berkeley: University of California Press, 1978

3. Crickmore, Paul F. *The Story of the Blackbirds: Lockheed's Skunk Works and the U-2/SR-71 Family of Reconnaissance Aircraft.* Osprey Publishing, 1989.

4. Carpenter, Gail A., and Stephen Grossberg. *The ART of Adaptive Pattern Recognition by a Self-Organizing Neural Network.* Computer 21, no. 3, 1988

CHAPTER 11: Planning, Control, and Communications

1. Ohno, Taiichi. *Toyota Production System: Beyond Large-Scale Production.* Productivity Press, 1988.

2. Hegel, Georg Wilhelm Friedrich. *Phenomenology of Spirit (1807).* Translated by G.M.A. Grube. Oxford University Press, 1977

CHAPTER 12: Deciding and Acting More Intelligently

1. Taylor, F., *The Principles of Scientific Management.* Harper & Brothers, 1911

2. Weber, Max. Economy and Society: *An Outline of Interpretive Sociology.* Berkeley: University of California Press, 1978

3. Drucker, Peter F. *The Age of Discontinuity: Guidelines to Our Changing Society.* New York: Harper & Row, 1969

4. Mintzberg, Henry. *The Structuring of Organizations.* Englewood Cliffs, NJ: Prentice-Hall, 1979

5. Waterman, Robert H., Jr. *In Search of Excellence: Lessons from America's Best-Run Companies.* New York: Harper & Row, 1982

6. Morita, Akio. *Made in Japan: Akio Morita and Sony.* New York: Dutton, 1986

7. Shakespeare, William. *Twelfth Night.* London: Thomas Nelson and Sons Ltd, 1601.

8. Cervantes Saavedra, Miguel de. *Don Quixote.* Translated by J. M. Cohen. New York: Everyman's Library, 1992

Conclusion: A Never-Ending Journey?

1. Musashi, Miyamoto. *The Book of Five Rings.* Translated by Victor Harris. London: Overlook Press, 1974.

Epilogue: 2023 Reflections

1. Cicero, Marcus Tullius. *De Oratore.* Translated by E.W. Sutton and H. Rackham. Cambridge, MA: Harvard University Press, 1942
2. Turteltaub, Jon, director. *Disney's The Kid.* Walt Disney Pictures, 2000
3. McKinsey Global Institute. *The State of AI in 2023: Generative AI's Breakout Year.* McKinsey & Company, 2023

Additional References

1. Ashby, W. Ross. *An Introduction to Cybernetics.* London: Chapman & Hall, 1956

2. Butler, R., *Designing Organizations: A Decision-Making Perspective,* New Jersey: Routledge, 1991

3. Chang-Tseh, H., *Some Potential Applications of Artificial Neural Systems in Financial Management,* Journal of Systems Management, April 1993

4. Cohen, M., *Individual Learning and Organizational Routine: Emerging Connections,* Organization Science, Volume 2, No. 1, February 1991

5. Drucker, Peter F. *The Age of Discontinuity: Guidelines to Our Changing Society.* Harper & Row, 1969

6. Forrester, J. and Doman, A., *The CEO as Organization Designer,* The McKinsey Quarterly, Volume 2, 1992

7. Garrat, B., *Creating a Learning Organisation,* London: Simon & Schuster, 1990

8. Herbert A. Simon, *The New Science of Management Decision,* Englewood Cliffs, New Jersey: Prentice-Hall, 1960

9. Herbert A. Simon, *The Sciences of the Artificial,* Cambridge, Massachusetts: MIT Press, 1969

10. March, James G., and Herbert A. Simon. Organizations. New York: Wiley, 1958

11. McAteer, P., *Simulations: Learning Tools for the 1990s,* Training & Development, Volume 45, October 1991

12. McGill, M., Slocum, J., and Lei, D., *Management Practices in Learning Organizations,* Organizational Dynamics, Volume 21, June 1992

13. McKee, D., *An Organizational Learning Approach to Product Integration,* The Journal of Product Innovation Management, Volume 9, No. 3, Sep 1992

14. Mintzberg, Henry, *Designing Effective Organizations,* New Jersey: Prentice Hall, 1983

15. Mintzberg, Henry. *The Structuring of Organizations.* Prentice-Hall, 1979.

16. Nonaka, I., *The Knowledge-Creating Company,* Harvard Business Review, Volume 69, December 1991

17. Normann, R., *Developing Capabilities for Organizational Learning,* In J. Pennings and others, Organizational Strategy and Change, San Francisco, California: Jossey-Bass Publishers, 1985

18. Schonberger, R., *Building a Chain of Customers,* New York, New York: The Free Press, 1992

19. Walsh, J. and Rivera, G., *'Organizational Memory',* Academy of Management Review, Volume 16, January 1991

20. Wiener, Norbert. *Cybernetics: Or Control and Communication in the Animal and the Machine.* Cambridge, MA: MIT Press, 1948

21. Wiston, P., *Artificial Intelligence,* Second Edition, New York, New York: Addison Wesley, 1991

22. Zornetzer, S., *Neural Networks,* New York, New York: Academic Press, 1990

23. Sagan, Carl. *Cosmos.* 1st ed. New York: Random House, 1980.

Index

About the Author

Alejandro (Alex) Picos is a Global Executive focusing product innovation through technology, focusing on AI, Advanced Analytics, and Big Data. He created Enterprise Data Services, PayPal's new Global Data, Analytics, and RegTech Capability and operated it as CDAO. This involved designing the largest global 'Big Data', Analytics, and Regulatory Oversight platform in Fintech, enhancing services for 350 million clients and 20 million merchants. The stack features innovative AI-driven solutions in MIS, Privacy, AML, Regulatory Reporting, XAI, and Consumer Data Sharing, resulting in several US patents. As a leader, Alex is fond of growing with teams that deliver quality and safe AI innovation, within the Silicon Valley ecosystem or elsewhere.

Prior to PayPal, Alex held CXO leadership roles in Banking at Citibank, Santander, and Fannie Mae. At Citibank, as Managing Director for Global Transformation, he improved consumer experiences across 38 countries. His career also includes a significant tenure as a Partner at McKinsey, where he led multiple Fintech launches co-founding the Technology Office, now known as McKinsey Digital.

Alex is multilingual, fluent in English, Portuguese, and Spanish. He holds an MBA with honors from IESA, a *summa cum laude* degree in Electronics Engineering from USB, and has completed exchange studies at Cornell University and AI extension studies at Stanford University.

A committed supporter of digital inclusion, Alex launched Intellixens to address the 'AI Divide', focusing on accelerating strategies and products centered around Generative AI. He has been a contributor to FELABAN *(Latin American Banking Association)* and FIBA *(Financial and International Banking Association)* since the dawn of digital banking.

Dedicated to the safe integration of Collaborative Human-Artificial Intelligence (ChAI™), Alex recently established a non-profit organization *(Safe ChAI Institute)*, aiming to make a contribution to pave our way toward a positive General AI discontinuity future.

271